C.S. Lewis Called Him Master

Exploring the Life & Adult Fantasy Works of
George MacDonald

by
Charles Seper

Victor, Broadstreet & Johnson Publishing/Chicago

C.S. LEWIS CALLED HIM MASTER

Printed in the USA by Victor, Broadstreet & Johnson Publishing.

First Edition

Includes bibliographical references: p.

ISBN: 978-0-6151-4907-3

Also see on the web: georgemacdonald.info

GEORGE MACDONALD

Contents

Chapter 1 The Sunny Land of Common Sense.........1

Chapter 2 *Phantastes*...8

Chapter 3 The Life...33

Chapter 4 The Un-Fundamentalist......................51

Chapter 5 *Lilith*...68

Chapter 6 The Devil Has His Day......................126

George MacDonald, 1824-1905

GEORGE MACDONALD

Preface

My first experience reading George MacDonald was a novella called *The Portent*. I had known beforehand that MacDonald was once a Scottish country preacher and that his story would likely contain something of the metaphysical as well as moralistic musings. What I wasn't prepared for was his great and proper (in my opinion) use of paranormal happenings in the lives of good and saintly characters. When modern readers come upon passages in contemporary stories dealing with individuals who suggest paranormal abilities, or similar characters in ancient books for that matter, words such as crazy, imbalanced, or even psychotic often come to their minds. Reading MacDonald is a very different and extraordinary experience however. He had the unique capacity of being able to convey how very normal, how rational, how sane through and through his characters were. It's those modern, skeptical minds that are made to feel inadequate in the wake. His characters didn't have distortions of the brain but contortions of the spirit. They wandered through "regions of the human heart", but these were very real places to MacDonald, at least as real as heaven or hell is to most Christians.

C.S. LEWIS CALLED HIM MASTER

While MacDonald has had a profound impact on my thoughts, I've tried to keep myself out of this book with the exception of a scant few footnotes. Obviously the suggestions made or conclusions reached while trying to identify literary symbols and metaphors in his works are mostly my own, and that's a great deal of why I wrote the book. MacDonald's fantasy literature is so full of symbolism, twofold meanings in parable-like storylines, and literary references to both his contemporaries and long forgotten writers, that almost everyone comes away bewildered after reading him for the first time. This is true even with some of his children's tales such as *The Golden Key* or *The Shadows*. Here I chose to keep my work short and focus on his only two fantasy novels written for adults: *Phantastes* and *Lilith*. I doubt that any man or woman has ever come close to figuring out every hidden detail in these stories, and I certainly make no such claim for myself. Nor is it of any great importance to know the meanings behind these things. While the symbolism may be fun to wrestle with, it's the spiritual wisdom he imparts that's of the greatest significance to us. Sometimes however, understanding the symbology may help the reader to better understand the message. I hope to help toward that end but always with the message in mind more than the metaphors involved which are purely a means to an end. In so doing, I have done my best to provide some kind of sensible guide toward understanding much of his written words in these two novels. As to the thoughts behind those words—they've been the subject of much ill-conceived Freudian and Jungian interpretations for the past one hundred or more years. There are few greater crimes that can be committed by modern biographers against their subjects. The over-interest in sexuality by today's literary researchers has been nothing short of astonishing and may very likely tell us more about the mind and morality of the biographers than their subjects. It is unfortunate that George MacDonald has not been exempt from this kind of analysis. If there was one trait which the people who knew MacDonald best, spoke of the most, it was his exemplary lifestyle. Readers who are imagining decadent, suggestive messages in a George MacDonald tale are doing themselves as great an injustice as they are MacDonald.

Although this isn't meant to be a biography per se, I will also try to give what I believe are the most pertinent details about George MacDonald's life. While there are specific chapters given to his life, and others to *Lilith* and *Phantastes*, the reader will find many facets of both in all the chapters. Neither are discussed in any sort of sequential order of events. I've allowed my thoughts to flow freely in a stream of consciousness sort of way.

Several biographies have been written on the life and times of George MacDonald over the years. However, the two written by his sons, Ronald and Greville, are still far and away the best and the only essential ones in my mind. If a reader would still like more detail on MacDonald's life after reading this book, I would suggest they find a copy of these two biographies. The first was a rather short essay of only 58-pages by Ronald MacDonald called *George MacDonald: A Personal Note*, that appeared in 1911 along with several other essays on Scottish topics in a book entitled *From a Northern Window: Papers, Critical, Historical and Imaginative*. This book has been out of print for several decades. Michael Phillips, however, repackaged the essay unaccompanied in book form in 1989 under the title *From a Northern Window: A Personal Reminiscence of George MacDonald by his Son*. As of this moment that book is also out of print, but used copies are easy to come by. The other biography, by Greville MacDonald, is *George MacDonald and his Wife*. That volume is currently available through Johannesen Printing and Publishing, a small company in Whitehorn, CA that makes wonderful hardbound, Smyth sewn reprints of books by and about George MacDonald. The only additional biographies, commentaries, or other books concerning George MacDonald I can heartily recommend are those written by Glen

Sadler. His knowledge of MacDonald's work is nothing short of extraordinary.

Whether I've managed to bring out anything of new significance, or correct some mistakes in judgment or substance by those who have gone before me, will be for the reader to decide. This is, after all, the man whom C.S. Lewis referred to as his master, and whom G.K. Chesterton called one of the three or four greatest men of the 19th century. But my goal with this book is not to elicit the praise and admiration of MacDonald scholars. Whether scholars will find anything new or useful here I cannot say. What I *do* hope to accomplish to some degree, with the help of George MacDonald, is to bridge a three way gap between those Christian Protestants who know little or nothing about the mystic life, the Roman Catholic and Eastern Orthodox branches of Christianity who do know at least a little, and the outsiders—the true mystics who so often feel themselves, because of a lack of understanding, to be in a sort of exile from much of greater Christendom. I don't know that I can say whole heartedly that George MacDonald was himself a mystic. He of course never admitted to being one. But then, that's the oddity about mystics—anyone who tells you that he is a mystic is almost certainly not one. They may be a thousand other things, but they are no mystic. It's as though they feel they're breaking some sort of sacred trust by admitting to having experienced the divine in this otherworldly manner, and they choose instead to speak in metaphors about these occurrences. So, while we can't say for certain that MacDonald had a mystical encounter of his own, we can however say that he wrote like one who had breathed the air of other worlds, and it's difficult to think of him in any other capacity after having read him. And while the British Isles were ensconced in Spiritualism and all the magical and occult trappings it often led to during MacDonald's lifetime, he seemed to have little regard, and at times even a great disdain, for such things despite the fact that many of his closest friends did participate in them.

GEORGE MACDONALD

George MacDonald's stories were in fact often written with these friends in mind as a way of reaching out to them spiritually using the props of Spiritualism and occult-like accouterments just as Charles Williams would do decades later with his tales—something many Christians have never understood.

The word mystic has been the subject of much misuse for nearly 200-years, mostly thanks to Spiritualist groups and occult writers. It is now often used to describe any sort of otherworldly event from the out of body experience (OBE) to astral projection, or even contact with devils or the dead. But this is a far cry from how the word was originally intended for use, and it is certainly not what George MacDonald generally meant when he used it. Many Christians today, especially Protestants, have no notion of who or what the great Christian Mystics were/are. In bygone days when the word mystic was used to refer to someone, it was always a reference to somebody who had had an encounter with the Divine, whether a voice from heaven or an angelic presence seen, heard, or felt. The Apostle Paul is often cited as the first mystic probably because of his reference to a man he knew that had an experience of being, "caught up to the third heavens", and because many scholars and theologians doing some major straw grasping want to believe that Paul was referring to himself although too modest to acknowledge it. They seem to set aside the fact that he wasn't shy at all in admitting other extraordinary religious experiences which happened to him such as the vision and audition in which Jesus spoke to him while blinding him with a light, or the many miracles he spoke of performing. Actually, Abraham, Enoch, Moses, and Daniel all had many more mystical encounters than did St. Paul. Nevertheless, the term mystic should have a good connotation to it, not an evil one as it so often does when presented today.

Modern psychologists would like us to believe that such otherworldly events are somehow inflicted on us—*by us*—that

C.S. LEWIS CALLED HIM MASTER

we generate these things in our own minds and somehow rather *miraculously* without our knowledge of having done it to ourselves. They use one miracle to try to conquer another. MacDonald would have nothing of this sort of psychobabble. To discuss otherworldly happenings in MacDonald's stories by the dim light of psychoanalysis, rather than as the spiritual occurrences of another world breaking through, would be like rejecting a banana while eating the peel. It could probably be done—no rational man would do it. And with that in mind, I give you George MacDonald.

Charles Seper

Chapter 1
The Sunny Land of Common Sense

D
o you know where the word *phantasm* comes from? It comes from Plato's name and his notion that there was such a thing as objective reality but that the five senses of the body didn't pick it up correctly, so reality he thought, was a somewhat hazy world for all people. Reality is *fuzzy*.

William Shakespeare in *The Tempest* said:

> Our revels now are ended. These our actors,
> As I foretold you, were all spirits and
> Are melted into air, into thin air:
> And, like the baseless fabric of this vision,
> The cloud-capp'd towers, the gorgeous palaces,
> The solemn temples, the great globe itself,
> Ye all which it inherit, shall dissolve
> And, like this insubstantial pageant faded,
> Leave not a rack behind. We are such stuff
> As dreams are made on, and our little life
> Is rounded with a sleep.[1]

C.S. LEWIS CALLED HIM MASTER

Do we even know when we're asleep or when we're truly awake? Could the reality we experience when we're asleep be made of the same substance we experience when we're awake? Are the two somehow tied together by a fabric of consciousness that we intuit, yet don't quite understand? Is this world of sleep and dreams the spirit world that religions speak of? And are there just the two worlds? Could there be more, perhaps many? Are these other worlds just parallel dimensions of the one we experience when awake but running on their own separate, yet connected, time lines like a many faceted diamond?

It's a profound mystery. There are those who have spent most of their lives trying to comprehend this mystery, would-be magicians for instance, who think they can pull on the puppet-master's strings and change the world to their liking. The Magician first seeks out a way to access the spirit world, to glimpse its inner workings and hopefully to converse with those who reside there. He then goes out in search of relationships between these two worlds, and therein lies what he believes to be magical correspondences and the ability to control them. He, so often wrapped in his own lust for power, never for a moment considers that perhaps these are things he was never meant to understand, let alone control.

From Ronald Taylor's translation of *The Devil's Elixirs* by E.T.A. Hoffman:

> I came to feel that what we call simply dream and imagination might represent the secret thread that runs through our lives and links its varied facets; and that the man who thinks that, because he has perceived this, he has acquired the power to break the thread and challenge that mysterious force which rules us, is to be given up as lost.[2]

GEORGE MACDONALD

There are also those, like Abraham or Daniel of the bible, whom the world has found it reasonable to refer to as the mystic, that is, someone who has had direct contact with the divine, yet not through their own initiation, but rather, because the divinity drew them in. And like the magician, the mystic also walks in two worlds following a trail of breadcrumbs, never knowing for sure where it will lead. But unlike the magician, the mystic never went out in search of breadcrumbs. The trail came looking for him. And that trail, Abraham and others like him, referred to as *The Word Of The Lord*.

We can't, of course, know what the ancients meant by that phrase. We do know that, like many spiritual words and phraseology we find in the bible, that the earliest known use of them came from the Sumerians who were in all likelihood the forefathers of Abraham's family. But in searching out the Sumerian writings we still don't get any solid notion of what was meant when they referred to the word of the Lord. Sometimes it may seem the Jews and the Sumerians both meant something akin to an actual voice discernable to the ears. Other times they seem to be talking about a kind of intuition—an inner knowledge. And still other times they seem to be recounting a dreamlike vision full of things that they don't quite understand. The language of the angels would seem to be that of symbolism and metaphor. This is most often the language of dreams and ... the language spoken in the land between the worlds, that place known to Romantic authors as the land of fairy (or faerie). And when writers try to communicate the knowledge of this enchanted land they often communicate it in the same form in which they received it. Perhaps they do this because they simply know no other way of expressing that which they themselves never fully comprehend.

George MacDonald, known best today for his fairytales, both for children and adults, said:

3

C.S. LEWIS CALLED HIM MASTER

The Greatest forces lie in the region of the uncomprehended.

...The best thing you can do for your fellow, next to rousing his conscience, is—not to give him things to think about, but to wake things up that are in him; or say, to make him think things for himself.[3]

He goes on to say that Nature rouses that *something* which is, "...deeper than the understanding—the power that underlies thought."[4]

Friedrich Hollander saw fairy stories as nothing more than an escape from reality, which in all likelihood is probably the way most people see them, especially those who haven't yet discovered MacDonald. Hollander said in *Munchhausen*:

Truth is hard and tough as nails
That's why we need fairy tales.[5]

Hollander had a great sense of humor, though frankly, he just didn't get it. But someone who did get it was one of the most prolific writers since Aristotle—G.K. Chesterton.

From his book, *Orthodoxy*, he says:

My first and last philosophy ... I learnt in the nursery... The things I believed then, the things I believe most now, are the things called fairy tales... They are not fantasies: compared with them other things are fantastic... Fairyland is nothing but the sunny country of common sense. It is not earth that judges heaven, but heaven that judges earth ... I knew the magic beanstalk before I tasted beans; I was sure of the Man in the Moon before I was certain of the moon.

GEORGE MACDONALD

I am concerned with a certain way of looking at life, which was created in me by the fairy tales, but has since been meekly ratified by the mere facts.[6]

One of those fairytales meant more to him than all the rest. It was to have a lasting impact on every part of his life. He spoke of it in the introduction to Greville MacDonald's biography of his father, George:

But in a certain rather special sense I for one can really testify to a book that has made a difference to my whole existence, which helped me to see things in a certain way from the start; a vision of things which even so real a revolution as a change of religious allegiance has substantially only crowned and confirmed. Of all the stories I ever read ... it remains the most real, the most realistic, in the exact sense of the phrase the most like life. It is called *The Princess and the Goblin*, and is by George MacDonald....[7]

....

And when he comes to be more carefully studied as a mystic, as I think he will be when people discover the possibility of collecting jewels scattered in a rather irregular setting, it will be found, I fancy, that he stands for a rather important turning point in the history of Christendom, as representing the particular Christian nation of the Scots. As protestants speak of the morning stars of the reformation, we may be allowed to note such names here and there as morning stars of the reunion.[8]

George MacDonald had a profound effect on his readers. Oddly, while he is best remembered today for his fantasy tales, materialism had a terrible, strong hold on the inhabitants of the 19th century, and so, it was his novels that made him popular in his own day. But even in his novels the reader will find a strong

5

touch of the metaphysical that so dominated his thoughts. MacDonald drew an enjoyment from reading books even as a young boy that encompassed all the typical poetic elements of elusiveness that so engage the mystical minded. By his late teens, as a student at King's College in Aberdeen, young George was already reading Shelley, Coleridge, James Hogg, and Tom Moore while also finding time to write poetry of his own. He had a powerful intellect, winning 3rd prize in Chemistry and 4th in Natural Philosophy, subjects he would lecture on years later at a Ladies' College to earn some much needed money. For a time he seriously considered going into medicine, but lack of funds forced him to retire the notion, and instead he devoted his energy to literature and languages. In time, having graduating with his Master of Arts, but still having no clear cut career choice, he decided to enter Highbury College where he would try his hand at theology. After two years there, he finally set upon what would seem to be his rightful course in life, that of a church minister.

It must be said that the majority of the people in his congregations took to the young preacher. However, his conscience would never allow him to speak anything he believed to be untrue, especially regarding God, the bible, or the faith, and so, he found himself at odds with clergymen and deacons nearly everywhere he tried to preach in these early days, mainly because of his anti-Calvinistic stance and what some thought to be at least a somewhat Universalistic outlook. MacDonald Only lasted around two years as a fulltime preacher. During this time, however, he had his first book published. *Within and Without*, a book length poem, appeared in 1855. George MacDonald was thirty one. And while it may seem that all his years of schooling had failed to bring him a substantial income, it was at least becoming clear what the future had in mind for him. In 1857 he had a second book of poetry published, but in 1858 his groundbreaking fairytale for adults—*Phantastes*—met with great success and finally put him on the map as a fiction writer. The map would have to adjust.

Chapter 2

Phantastes (*A Faerie Romance for Men and Women*)

C.S. Lewis, the author of *The Screwtape Letters*, *The Chronicles of Narnia*, *Out of the Silent Planet* and several other classics, regarded MacDonald in as high esteem as one author can hold another. He quoted from him in nearly every book he wrote even putting together, *George MacDonald an Anthology*, taken mostly from MacDonald's religious writings.

It was *Phantastes* that first introduced Lewis to MacDonald. He spoke of it in the introduction to his anthology:

> It must be more than thirty years ago that I bought—almost unwillingly, for I had looked at the volume on that bookstall and rejected it on a dozen previous occasions—the Everyman edition of *Phantastes*. A few hours later I knew I had crossed a great frontier... What it actually did to me was to convert, even to baptize ... my imagination.[1]

Phantastes opens with a quote from Novalis, part of which says:

GEORGE MACDONALD

One can imagine stories without rational cohesion and yet filled with associations, like dreams, and poems ... full of beautiful words, but also without rational sense and connections ....

....

In a genuine fairy-story, everything must be miraculous, mysterious, and interrelated, everything must be alive, each in its own way.[2]

Phantastes is a book full of stories that would be disconnected from one another with the exception that one person, Anodos, is a part of them all just as we are always within our dreams however detached they may seem. Anodos is the central character of *Phantastes*. He arrives in the land of fairy by way of awakening in the morning after his twenty first birthday to find that his surroundings are much different than that to which he is accustomed to seeing in his bedroom. A stream is running through it now, and a path by the stream rambles to a wooded area. Anodos gets up and washes in the stream. Other events in the story lead us to surmise some time later that this washing may symbolize an important event. The young man decides to follow the path into the woods, but interestingly, when he gets to the tree line he leaves the path and instead forges his own way through the woods, all the while, chastising himself for having done so because his instincts were telling him to stay to the path. Later in the story, Anodos follows another stream into a castle:

According to my custom since I first entered Fairy Land, of taking for a guide whatever I first found moving in any direction, I followed the stream from the basin of the fountain. It led me to a great open door ....[3]

C.S. LEWIS CALLED HIM MASTER

Anodos, by the way, is from the Greek and can mean several things pertaining to a *path*, but in this case MacDonald makes use of the clearest general meaning of the word—*without a path*.

The young wanderer will spend many days in this new world meeting along the way several inhabitants of the land, the most important of which are women, and one thing that is most particularly neither man nor woman, but a shadow, a shadow which is very persistent in its pursuit of Anodos. Just prior to this Anodos is put back onto the path by the tenants of a small cottage in the woods, but after meeting the shadow he is seized with terror and thinks no longer of the path, but of fleeing the shadow. This shade is no different than the mirror image we all have while standing in the sun except this particular silhouette heeds no consideration as to the sun's position or even cares if there is a sun. It is simply unrelenting. The gloomy darkness which Anodos refers to as his, "demon shadow", plays the role of a deceiver. It suggests the things he sees in the fairy world are something different than they really are and even hides things from his vision.

As his days unfold in this strange land, Anodos, by the help of the many strangers he meets upon the way, would learn, by and by, to follow the paths they locate for him. This comes at the price of losing his pride, and as the final strands of his pride disappear, so does the image of his shadowy companion. One of the strangers Anodos meets in this country is a knight whose rusty armor is, bit by bit, made clean from the blows of noble battles. This provides us with a secondary metaphor that is symbolic of losing one's pride. At its heart that is what this story is about. And, it is essentially what the majority of all great tales have to teach us. They're directions for the cleaning up of the soul and of the soul's chief source of decay—pride.

There was still, and always would be, a big part of the country parson in George MacDonald, yet one gets nothing of the self-aggrandizing or ostentatious manner in his personal life, nor in his novels, that we've come to associate with many sermonizers in our day. We instead find a humble man whipping his soul into shape and giving us a glimpse of the process through his own stories. And indeed we find—as his son, Greville, attests to—that MacDonald often wrote his personal experiences into his stories, not only the occurrences of everyday life, but from his deeper metaphysical questions concerning God and the workings of the world, even those coming from the cusp of reality. He says in a letter to his uncle, James MacDonald:

> ...the conviction is, I think, growing upon me that the smallest events are ordered for us, while yet in perfect consistency with the ordinary course of cause and effect in the world. I am strongly inclined to think that whatever has a moral effect of any kind on our minds, God manages for us ... How far the events of those who do not at all seek to serve Him are controlled by him ... is a question about which I have no opinion at all—at least not a settled one.[4]

That reads very much like the typical, ordinary, everyday thoughts of a mystic, someone whose mind is always tearing away at the veil of materialism. And it takes a mystical kind of mind to both hear and to follow—the word of the Lord. It's a mind that's always listening, always at work intuiting the deeper things within the sphere of his/her existence. MacDonald almost seems to embrace quietism in a passage from his novel, *What's Mines, Mine.*

> When you have got quite alone, sit down and be lonely ... fold your hands in your lap, and be still. Do not try to think anything ... by and by, it may be, you will begin to know something of nature. Nature will soon

speak to you, or not until, as Henry Vaughn says, some
veil be broken in you.[5]

The ancient inhabitants of Mesopotamia weren't the only
ones to have no clear notion as to what that term—the word of
the Lord—meant. Theologians have disagreed for 2,000-years as
to what it signifies when presented in biblical passages. Some
say it refers to the Torah only (the first five books of the bible).
Some say it refers specifically to prophecies that designate
themselves as being the word of the Lord. Others say that New
Testament authors were speaking of the Septuagint (the Greek
version of the Old Testament) since that's what they most likely
used and quoted from most often. Still others point to the ten
commandments. And most importantly of all, Jesus, the Word
that became a living, breathing human representing God
himself within the cosmic play—*The Book of Life*. It may be that
all are correct to some degree. We may, however, find in
MacDonald something that suggests a new way of envisioning
this phrase.

When Abraham heard the word of the Lord, he was told,
or perhaps intuited, that he was to, "Get up and go to a land
that I will show you." We can't help but wonder if he even had
any notion as to which direction he was to set off in. The text
mentions nothing of how Abraham was to find his way to this
new place. Yet he does find it. How? We may surmise that
Abraham followed the natural course of events in his daily life,
that he traveled the route that made itself available to him, that
he listened to an inner voice while following outward signs.
This is exactly what Anodos does in *Phantastes*. And, when he
begins to meander off-course, a situation will present itself that
tells him he's off-track, and a better path-choice will open up to
him. We may suggest here that MacDonald is trying with his
novel to teach us a new meaning of—the word of the Lord. It is
very simply—a path. It is a path full of symbolic meanings in
everyday occurrences, a path with obstacles that must be

traversed, a path with choices that await our choosing, and with those choices comes the fashioning of our character.

Pilgrim's Progress was a story that set a mold for followers of the path. It's a prototype that's been adhered to by most great authors at some point in their lives ever since. It's the idea of a voyager taking a journey and what happens to him along the way. Or, perhaps we should rather say, what he learns and becomes while navigating the path. C.S. Lewis used this mold for almost every story he wrote. His characters were nearly always going places, having adventures along the way, and building character in the process whether they were traveling to Mars, Venus, Narnia, or taking a bus ride through Purgatory. It's no surprise that we find his literary father, George MacDonald, also employing this same storybook device so very often. He tells of people traveling through dream worlds, taking trips through mirrors to strange lands, following a silver thread through mountain caves, and even traveling to the back of the north wind. Obedience to one's conscience is at the heart of the journey *and* a willingness to be led.

From Volume 2 of *Unspoken Sermons* MacDonald says, "Obedience is the joining of the links of the eternal round. Obedience is but the other side of the creative will. Will is God's will, obedience is man's will; the two make one."[6]

It's when Anodos learns to play his role in the eternal round that his journey finally comes to an end.

If we think of—the word of the Lord—as being merely a literary work, a particular bible for instance, or the Torah (as many Jews do in fact believe), we are left with something that may be a great help to us in our most cogent hours of study and reflection, yet something utterly devoid of value at other moments. If we're lost in a cave no bible will tell us which passage to take. Nor will the Torah tell you which direction is north in a land of darkness beneath the earth. It's in these hours of desperation that the word of the Lord takes on a greater meaning for us and something more personal as well. Holy books are written for the many. Intuiting the voice of God, a voice not of reason but simply of direction, is a personal experience that comes with making a choice, whether choosing a passage in a cave, a mate, a career, or a home. In a nutshell, it's the bequest of wisdom. We may sometimes find several choices available to us at times that seem equally agreeable or disagreeable, with no clear way of deciding between them. Here we may do well to follow MacDonald's advice to: "fold your hands in your lap, and be still ... until ... some veil be broken in you." C.S. Lewis takes the passage in a cave metaphor to an unimaginable level in his sci-fi novel, *Perelandra*.

One of the more fascinating elements in *Phantastes* is the castle. If there are any real (non-ghosts) inhabitants in this castle we never learn of them, save one, the wife of the rusty knight, and this Anodos doesn't learn until long after he has left the dwelling, although he does seem to realize that this woman, who he earlier freed from a magical enchantment where she had been turned to stone and now is a statue once again, is something far removed from the other spirits he sees glimpses of now and then. MacDonald's fantasy stories always involve spiritual beings of various sorts. He doesn't seem to rely on the works of past authors much in developing his spirits. More often than not we aren't told *what* they are. There are seldom any mention of the varying degrees of angels for instance. In his children's tales there are *sometimes* ogres, goblins, fairy godmothers, and other familiar names, but it's an exception when he actually names the creatures. More often he simply describes their look and their actions and leaves the rest to the reader's thoughts. The inhabitants of the castle appear to be something along the line of ghosts, but these aren't ghosts as we're used to hearing them described by other authors. MacDonald's ghosts are more like dream characters where anything is possible, where they can be without faces, or be nothing but a skeleton. We're not entirely sure if they are in any way human or if they have ever lived in the material world at all. His spirits seldom are about the business of scaring. His ghosts may dance in ballrooms or freeze and become hard as rock statues the minute a living person enters a room. Sometimes they're heard talking or laughing but are not seen. They are very much like the inhabitants of dreams where they move and produce a visual display of a sort, yet have an existence whose purpose is vague at best. The castle is full of just such residents as this.

Within the castle Anodos finds a library that has a certain enchantment about it. When he reads the stories in the books, he finds that he himself is a component of the stories, that he is really there and taking a part in things.

> Or if the book was one of travels, I found myself the traveler... Was it history? I was the chief actor therein... With a fiction it was the same. Mine was the whole story. For I took the place of the character who was most like myself, and his story was mine; until ... I would awake, with a sudden bewilderment, to the consciousness of my present life, recognizing the walls and roof around me ....[7]

Anodos goes on to relate two of the stories he read there. One is a chronicle of life in another world on a whole different sort of planet with a very different set of planetary laws—an inhabited planet older than the Earth. The other is a love story revolving around an enchanted mirror. What we gain from these two stories, aside from their moral statements, is a very good insight to MacDonald's levelheaded approach concerning the differences and yet similarities between the true mystics and those simply dabbling in occult affairs. He starts off the first tale:

> They who believe in the influences of the stars over the fates of men, are, in feeling at least, nearer the

truth than they who regard the heavenly bodies as related to them merely by a common obedience to an external law. All that man sees has to do with man. Worlds cannot be without an intermundane relationship. The community of the centre of all creation suggests an interradiating connection and dependence of the parts. Else a grander idea is conceivable than that which is already embodied. The blank, which is only a forgotten life, lying behind the consciousness, and the misty splendour, which is an undeveloped life, lying before it, may be full of mysterious revelations of other connexions with the worlds around us, than those of science and poetry. No shining belt or gleaming moon, no red and green glory in a self-encircling twin star, but has a relation with the hidden things of a man's soul, and, it may be, with the secret history of his body as well. They are portions of the living house wherein he abides.[8]

MacDonald, though himself a great student (and teacher) of science, has that mystical sense within him that there is obviously much more to life, and to man, than meets the eye. And he realizes that people far from his own religious convictions may still find the interconnectedness of all objects which take up space, as well as those (namely—souls) which do not. Therefore, while he may not condone the practice, it is no wonder to him that those who seek out meaning within the movement of the stars, or the position of sticks or tea leaves, may well find something of purpose within those techniques. In the concluding sentence of this paragraph, he appears to hint at a belief common to mystics the world over in every religion that says all things which take up existence do so within the eternal mind of the Creator, or as St. Paul says (quoting Epimenides), "For in Him we live and move and have our being." We also find Paul stating in the same paragraph that God left little or

GEORGE MACDONALD

nothing to chance, that He set the times and places for men to live. If the Jews had a word for *coincidence* in those days we find nothing like it in any bible. That the world is full of complexity and yet we have free will within it, and still more, that we find apparent chaos on the subatomic level within things like atomic foam, is something that will always baffle mankind. It's easy to see why Chesterton thought God to be a being of great "mirth". MacDonald takes no surprise at the thought of an astrologist finding patterns within the stars and the lives of men. He takes no astonishment of it because he knows that such things are bound to be so, and that they are but small graces really. That is, that they may be sufficient to point such individuals (those who practice seeing the future) to the world of spirit, and in doing so, may at least open their minds to something that is greater than themselves. In the end, he also knows that while there are connections to be made in life, there is also sufficient chaos to keep men from knowing the truly deep things of God. God built the world with a foolproof failsafe device to keep out prying eyes and prying minds. Men may be able to look so far ... but no farther. He wishes them not to look at all, but rather, to seek out the face of their Creator, and in so doing, greater truths may be made known. This is the life of the mystic (perhaps the truest kind of saint). The mystic seeks only to know and to please his God and cares nothing for the knowledge that leads to power. The magician is on an opposite path, seeking to control his own destiny, which ... brings us to the other story from the great library Anodos will narrate for us.

The second tale is undoubtedly one of the best yarns MacDonald ever spun. If you've read *Phantastes* already then you know that the synopsis Anodos gives of each tale is nothing less than two short stories. In the second we discover a young man, Cosmo, who buys a mirror only to find later that it has an enchantment. When he brings the mirror home and gazes into it for the first time, he sees a beautiful woman come into his room and lay upon his couch/bed. He sees this in the mirror;

17

however, when he turns to look at the couch, the woman is not there. She exists only within the looking glass. Every night she comes and is gone before morning, and every night he grows impassioned to have her in his arms. But, while he can see *her*, she cannot return his gaze, nor hear his voice. It is as though there are two identical rooms, each housing the man and the woman. Cosmo can see that the girl is troubled when she comes, as though she has been forced to do so.

One night she appears in the mirror dressed exquisitely, and Cosmo realizes that she has a life of her own during the day when she is not in the mirror. He begins to worry that she may have a lover somewhere, and this he cannot take. We're told early in the story that Cosmo has among his books several which deal with Alchemy (assumedly) and others that appear to be of the dark arts.

> These studies, besides those subjects necessary to his course at the University, embraced some less commonly known and approved; for in a secret drawer lay the works of Albertus Magnus and Cornelius Agrippa, along with others less read and more abstruse. As yet, however, he had followed these researches only from curiosity, and had turned them to no practical purpose.[9]

Up until this moment, Cosmo has had only a curiosity with magic. Now he has a temptation which urges him to practice what he had thus far only read about. He prepares several spells, forms a charmed circle, and begins his own enchantment which he hopes will bring the woman into his real room rather than the reflected room in the mirror. It works. The girl had more or less been sleepwalking every time she had entered the mirrored room—now she would come into the non-mirrored room, and fully awake. In doing so, she lets Cosmo know that she has been under a spell attached to the mirror and asks him to break it. But before he can, he blacks out. Later he assumes that some sort of magic/demoniac intervention was the cause (he had stepped out of the charmed circle). The girl and the mirror are both gone. Eventually he finds that another young man of ill-repute has gotten the mirror, likely from the same merchant from which Cosmo originally purchased it. Cosmo determines to get to the mirror and smash it. We aren't told the details of the events that transpire, but we are told that the lady is a Polish Princess, and that she suddenly awakens on her own bed from a trancelike condition (coma?) which she has been in for some days. She realizes that the enchantment has been broken and rushes out to find, and to thank, Cosmo. (Apparently he had found and broken the mirror). When she finds him, however, he is dying from a wound in his side and the story ends.

There are some oddities sprinkled throughout the tale and some curiosities left unanswered. When Cosmo magically brings the princess into his room and she sees him for the first time, she calls him by name. How does she know it? Earlier Cosmo finds himself repulsed by the shopkeeper who sells him the mirror: "In fact, now he looked closely at him for the first time, he felt a kind of repugnance to him, mingled with a strange feeling of doubt whether a man or a woman stood before him."[10]

We're led to believe that the shopkeeper was somehow connected to the enchantment of the mirror. As Cosmo begins to leave with the mirror the merchant says, "Sold for the sixth time! I wonder what will be the upshot of it this time. I should think my lady had enough of it by now!"[11]

With all the devilry involved amid enchantments and with the shopkeeper looking repulsive in some way along with having the look of one who is androgynous it must dawn on the reader that perhaps he is a fallen angel. (They are often described in ancient texts as looking androgynous). It's something that never becomes clear. We don't even have the name of the merchant or his shop.

At its heart this is the story of mankind searching for a love fulfilled. It's our story. The first of the library tales was of another world where the subject of soul mates was very predominate. In this second story we have the search for that soul mate. But having found the beloved (using my best Dante and Beatrice tone of voice) we realize that we cannot force the love of the "holy other". It must be offered freely to us. And again MacDonald lets us know that magical and occult associations will not gain for us that which our hearts long for. What we long for is the love of our Creator—to see his face. MacDonald uses romantic love as the setting for the search for fulfillment which all created beings strive for (whether they realize it or not) in many of his stories. His fondness for the Dante and Beatrice saga would stay with him for life and effect nearly everything he wrote.

He tells us at the beginning of this tale:

Of course, while I read it, I was Cosmo, and his history was mine. Yet, all the time, I seemed to have a kind of double consciousness, and the story a double meaning. Sometimes it seemed only to represent a simple story of ordinary life, perhaps almost of universal life; wherein two souls, loving each other and longing to come nearer, do, after all, but behold each other as in a glass darkly.[12]

He goes on to say:

Nay, how many who love never come nearer than to behold each other as in a mirror; seem to know and yet never know the inward life; never enter the other soul; and part at last, with but the vaguest notion of the universe on the borders of which they have been hovering for years?[13]

Those are some very intriguing words. Some believe that all romantic love is just a temporary retreat, and that the love we really long for is that of our Father/Creator. They say that all other loves are but provisional fixations that offer a little relief until the fount of love is made manifest before our anxious souls. And, when that day comes, "At the resurrection people will neither marry nor be given in marriage; they will be like the angels in heaven", our need for those provisional fixations will no longer be important to us. Now we gaze into that glass darkly. Later ....

Many of the ideas in this tale, particularly the sleepwalking woman, would later show up in MacDonald's short novel, *The Portent*.

One last note: the first time ever Cosmo gazes into the looking glass, sees the lady, and then realizes she exists only in the mirror, it has a powerful effect on him.

> He gazed till he was weary, and at last seated himself near the new-found shrine, and mechanically took up a book, like one who watches by a sick-bed. But his eyes gathered no thoughts from the page before him. His intellect had been stunned by the bold contradiction, to its face, of all its experience, and now lay passive, without assertion, or speculation, or even conscious astonishment; while his imagination sent one wild dream of blessedness after another coursing through his soul.[14]

Cosmo is a University student with a sharp mind and a taste for scholarship, but once he has a genuine encounter with the supernatural all of his previous notions about how the world works would, "now lay passive, without assertion, or speculation, or even conscious astonishment... " One can't help but be reminded of Thomas Aquinas and the story of how, while praying one day in his room, he had some kind of supernatural encounter of his own that made him say afterwards that even his most notable writings about God and the church seemed like rubbish. No matter how much we think we know about God, or the world at large, we often can't help but sense that we really know nothing at all. It principally remains a great mystery to us and we must be satisfied to settle for gazing through the glass darkly. MacDonald teaches us to be content with that.

George MacDonald entered King's College (formerly called St. Mary's) in 1840. It took him 5 years to earn a four year degree, having stayed out the 1842-43 school year probably due to a lack of funds. During this year he traveled somewhere in the far north and took up employment cataloguing a library at a castle or mansion, the location of which is unknown, but generally thought to be either Dunbeath or Thurso Castles. Greville surmises that these months spent working in the library may have been very important to his father.

Many of MacDonald's stories revolve heavily upon the use of a library, in particular *The Portent* and *Lilith* along with *Phantastes* of course, but he also made considerable use of a library in at least five other novels. In *The Portent*, he goes into some description of a library where the main character is also working at cataloguing books, and here he tells us:

> But I found in the library what I liked far better—many romances of a very marvelous sort, and plentiful interruption they gave to the formation of the catalogue. I likewise came upon a whole nest of the German classics ... I found in these volumes a mine of wealth inexhaustible.[15]

GEORGE MACDONALD

Greville supposes this to be at least somewhat autobiographical of his father's days spent working in the library and suggests that this library in the far north may be the place he first encountered the works of German author, E.T.A. Hoffmann. Hoffmann made what was possibly the earliest use of a doppelganger in a story, something MacDonald would also employ several times (although he was very likely just as influenced by the doppelganger in James Hogg's "The Private Memoirs and Confessions of a Justified Sinner", 1824. Hog—The Ettrick Shepherd—was not only one of MacDonald's favorite writers, but this was one of the best stories ever produced by a Scottish author). Here he may also have first come upon the writings of Friedrich von Hardenberg, better known as, Novalis, another German author, generally regarded as the father of Romanticism. MacDonald would later translate and publish at least twenty one of the poems of Novalis, but much more important to MacDonald would have been the two unfinished stories Novalis was writing at the time of his death. He made great use of sleep and dreams throughout them, and the influence on MacDonald's own tales is quickly discernable to anyone having read both. [For a very well done and yet short comparative of Novalis and MacDonald, I highly recommend finding a copy of Novalis's, *Hymns to the Night/Spiritual Songs*, translated by George MacDonald, published by Temple Lodge Publishing—1992 and reading the excellent afterward written by William Webb, to whom I am much in debt.]

....

It may be helpful for those readers who have never read his work if we look at a few lines from Novalis's *Hymns to the Night*.

Once when I was shedding bitter tears, when, dissolved in pain, my hope was melting away, and I stood alone by the barren hillock which in its narrow dark bosom hid the vanished form of my Life, lonely as never yet was lonely man, driven by anguish unspeakable ... then out of the blue distances, came a shiver of twilight, and at once snapped the bond of birth, the fetter of light. Away fled the glory of the world, and with it my mourning; the sadness flowed together into a new, unfathomable world. Thou soul of the Night, heavenly slumber, didst come upon me ... I saw the glorified face of my beloved. In her eyes eternity reposed. I laid hold of her hands ...Into the distance swept by, like a tempest, thousands of years... Never was such another dream; then first and ever since I hold fast an eternal, unchangeable faith in the heaven of the night, and its sun, the beloved.

....

Now I know when will come the last morning: when the light no more scares away Night and Love, when sleep shall be without waking, and but one continuous dream. I feel in me a celestial exhaustion. Long and weariful was my pilgrimage to the holy grave, and crushing was the cross. The crystal wave, which, imperceptible to the ordinary sense, springs in the dark bosom of the hillock against whose foot breaks the flood of the world, he who has tasted it, he who has stood on the mountain frontier of the world, and looked across into the new land, into the abode of the Night, verily he turns not again into the tumult of the world, into the land where dwells the Light in ceaseless unrest.

On those heights he builds for himself tabernacles—tabernacles of peace; there longs and loves and gazes across, until the welcomest of all hours draws him down into the waters of the spring. Afloat above remains what is earthly, and is swept back in storms; but what became holy by the touch of Love, runs free through hidden ways to the region beyond, where, like odours, it mingles with love asleep. Still wakest thou, cheerful Light, the weary man to his labor, and into me pourest gladsome life; but thou wilest me not away from Memory's moss-grown monument.

I live all the daytime
In faith and in might:
In holy rapture
I die every night.[16]

In the above passage from *Hymns of the Night*, Novalis is putting to verse his own personal vision wrought from his grief over the death of his very young fiancé, Sophie von Kuhn. The barren hillock he refers to is her grave. We don't know the mode of this visionary experience, whether he fell into an actual dream or a more trancelike state, but we do know that he had an experience that profoundly changed his life, making him a "new man", (from whence comes the term—Novalis) and that it contained in it that which he likened to the world of sleep, dreams, and the spiritual abode of man's true self.

Novalis died very young, not yet quite the age of twenty nine. His writing has in it that youthful mode that most young writers seem to have of being overdone more often than not. C.S. Lewis, who, while an enthusiast of MacDonald's fantasies, was overall, less than admirable of his other novels. In the preface to his MacDonald Anthology he stated that MacDonald's novels sometimes contained "...an over-sweetness picked up from Novalis." But just two paragraphs later he also went on to praise MacDonald and Novalis both saying that, while most myths were made in prehistoric times, "...every now and then there occurs in the modern world a genius—a Kafka or a Novalis—who can make such a story. MacDonald is the greatest genius of this kind whom I know."

Whether MacDonald first encountered the writing of Novalis in the library of the far north or elsewhere, it made its mark on his soul like a carving on a tombstone.

C.S. LEWIS CALLED HIM MASTER

...

Besides the library, Anodos spends much of his time at the castle within a great hall (actually several halls) full of statues that come to life and dance. There is written upon the pedestals the words, "TOUCH NOT!" But eventually Anodos figures out that one of the statues is the white marble lady he had freed in the forest earlier by singing to her, and now she is a statue once more. Somehow he discerns that if he sings to her again it will free her here as well. As he does so, she does indeed begin to take on a more lifelike look, but by the end of his song he can't resist embracing the statue, and when he does, the statue becomes the flesh and blood lady once again. She screams, "You should not have touched me!", and runs out of the castle. At the beginning of the book Anodos also tried to embrace the fairy from the desk and she said to him, "Foolish boy, if you could touch me, I should hurt you." So twice now he has been told not to touch two specific women from the world of fairy. Shortly we will hear it again.

After the white lady rushes from the castle, Anodos follows her out the door and has a sudden recognition that there is something different about this door from the others, they being made of ivory or ebony, but this one is, "...a heavy, rough door, altogether unlike any others I had seen in the palace ... this seemed of old oak, with heavy nails and iron studs."[17]

This door probably symbolizes a coffin. Beneath the door is written, *No one enters here without the leave of the queen.* He has no idea who this queen is (nor do we ever find out) but goes through the door anyway, and when he does, he steps outside the castle and finds himself in a countryside he doesn't recognize and the castle disappears, just as in dreams we may round a corner and find ourselves in a new dream world. He sees the lady go behind a large rock, and when he comes to the other side of it, he finds not the woman but a gaping hole in the earth, an entrance to a cave. This seems figurative of the woman's death and grave; the rock—her tombstone.

26

GEORGE MACDONALD

Now we must stop and ask ourselves about this a moment. The castle Anodos just came from may also seem to represent death. It's made completely of marble, and its whiteness gleams in the sun. It has a "chamber" in it marked with his name. It has no windows, and its description sounds almost like that of a great mausoleum, perhaps even something out of Egypt's Valley of the Kings. And all of its residents are statues, but statues, however, that seem to come to life at times. And there are spirit beings which Anodos can only see faint outlines of, like ghosts. So when Anodos opens the oak door, is he leaving a coffin or entering one?

According to Greek mythology, Hades and his queen, Persephone ruled the underworld where people went after death. In this underworld was a great palace from which they reigned. It was set in a field of visions and had many gates, which describes the palace in MacDonald's tale quite well. It also had many "guests", as did the palace in *Phantastes*. The underworld which eventually took on the name of its ruler, Hades, had two sections: Erebus, a more pleasant place, and Tartarus, a "deeper", more sinister area wherein dwelled hazy, indistinct spirits. And, flowing throughout Hades are many rivers; you'll recall that Anodos came to the castle by way of a river. It would appear that Anodos has entered Hades to bring back his marble lady, and at first entered Erebus, but now must follow her deeper down into Tartarus.

When he goes into the hole, what he sees there is very like the grim visions we should expect to see if we ever ended up in one of the nastier underworlds of the dead written about by the ancients. The question will dawn on the reader whether the marble lady is dead, or Anodos, or both? Why are they in the underworld unless they are dead? Anodos didn't, after all, intentionally go into the underworld to save her. He never even knew it was the underworld he was entering or knew the marble lady had entered it too. Interestingly, he never finds the woman there.

27

C.S. LEWIS CALLED HIM MASTER

When he eventually comes forth from the other end of the cavern he observes that he is now in the presence of a wintry, rocky seashore with icy winds and no other land in site. The cold spray of the sea and the chilling wind are even more desolating than the underworld from which he has just emerged. He can take no more and decides to end his life in the sea rather than allowing the sea to do it slowly of its own accord, "'I will not be tortured to death,' I cried; 'I will meet it half-way. The life within me is yet enough to bear me up to the face of Death, and then I die unconquered.'"[18]

But the sea will not have his death. He finds that he is pushed out of its depths to the surface of the waters by some mysterious force, whereupon a little boat is found floating beside him, and soon he is suspended in the lap of peace and contentment.

Shortly, Anodos ends up on an island and in the cottage of an ancient looking woman with very young eyes, a woman old and yet beautiful, one who is full of knowledge and wisdom and who often sits at a spinning wheel. For those who have read other of Macdonald's fantasies, this is no surprise. An old and wise woman much like the one described here shows up in many of them. This chapter—nineteen—may be the most intricate element found in *Phantastes*. When he first enters the cottage, the old woman sings a song that is a tale of a husband, wife, and child. The child had died some time earlier, and then, in her grief the mother died also. The husband, while in a dreamlike state, comes upon the dead wife, but she is transfigured into someone he no longer recognizes. Eventually he does come to know her, but she tells him that, HE MUST NOT TOUCH HER. After a time he forgets this, however, and embraces his ghost wife. Having done so, she seems to die yet again and is motionless.

So three times we have this strange warning not to touch a particular beautiful woman in the fairy world or something dire will happen. Yet there are other women whom Anodos is allowed to touch in this land. We learn by the tale's end that this is a part of the dying to self that he is learning. It's why he's been brought to the fairy world to begin with, and in this song he learns it yet again by observing another man going through the same test. We learn in life by observing and by doing. It often takes a great deal of both to drive home a point to us. There is continual death and rebirth in *Phantastes*, some of it symbolic, some actual. We are persistently reminded, like the ringing of a bell, of the words St. Paul wrote, "I die daily." In our lives a part of us is continually dying. Either the bad is driven from us, or the good, every hour, each to its death.

There are four doors corresponding to the four walls of this cottage and while our young traveler only enters through one of them, he at some point will go out through all four, and each time it takes him to a different world where he will forget about the old woman and her cottage for a time and have an adventure. He always manages to find his way back in the end though, when something sparks his memory of the place. Before Anodos ever goes out through any of the doors, he sleeps for a while, only to awaken and find the old woman acting as a seer while standing in front of each door successively. One door is a door of great distress where the woman weeps while standing before it. At another she stands and sighs. A third door finds her in fear and dismay. The final door makes her shudder and stand, "still as a statue", and statues generally signify the dead in *Phantastes*. The adventures Anodos has on the other side of these doors will correspond to the woman's emotional state while positioned before them. Some readers have suggested in the past that these four doors represent the four elementals: earth, air, water, and fire. But even if we take them in the corresponding states that sorcerers and occultists have named (something MacDonald would not likely have done): fertility, intelligence, emotions, and strength, this still makes very little sense in light of Anodos' adventures and the old woman's actions.

C.S. LEWIS CALLED HIM MASTER

If these four doors are symbolic of anything at all, it would appear more reasonable for them to correspond to something in MacDonald's Christian faith. This is especially true in light of the extreme comfort Anodos takes from the old woman. She is very much a comforter, and it would seem sensible for her to be a depiction of the Holy Spirit at work in our interior lives. The four doors may well symbolize various stages in the cross of Christ. Beyond the first door Anodos finds himself a young boy again and experiences the drowning death of his brother after a quarrel the night before, which is of course accompanied by much weeping. This may express the sadness and distress Jesus must have felt leading up to the last supper where he knows that his friend Judas has entered into spiritual death, aligning himself with darkness, and plotting to betray him; the same Judas who will later hang himself. The second door takes Anodos to his heart's desire, which is the white, marble lady. However, he then learns that she is married to the rusty knight he befriended earlier, and while Anodos must accept that the marble lady is not included in his destiny, he cannot help but to be very sad about it; thus it is a door of sighs and great disappointment. This could signify the incident of Jesus at the Garden of Gethsemane, where he prays for the cup to be taken from him but is not granted his desire, and in the end, becomes resolute about his fate. On the other side of the third door, Anodos will find himself in a mortuary chapel above the burial vault of his ancestors. He has no understanding of what is going on around him and is in total darkness and extreme fear. Eventually he cries out for help in his distress. We may connect this element of the story with the famous cry from the cross, "My God, my God, why have you forsaken me?" We know nothing of what happens at the final door except that it seems to represent the death of Anodos. The old lady in the cottage rescues him, however, and brings him back from this door called "timeless". The bible tells us that the Holy Spirit brings not only comfort but a myriad of "powers" to believers in

30

Christ including the resurrection of the dead. If the old woman is a representation of the Spirit of God, then her having the power of resurrection would make perfect sense to us. These are all obviously conjectures, however, and should not to be taken too seriously. The four doors, and the actions associated with them, may not represent anything at all other than the woman's abilities as God's seer sent to Anodos to teach, warn, and comfort him during his spiritual/interior travels in a world that is not of his own making, although psychologists—with little or no evidence—would suggest otherwise to us.

Anodos turned twenty one the day before he left for his journey, which lasted for twenty one days, and which he said felt like twenty one years. He learns obedience in the land of fairy and to be rid of self will. He tells us upon his return:

> I began the duties of my new position, somewhat instructed, I hoped, by the adventures that had befallen me in Fairy Land. Could I translate the experience of my travels there, into common life? This was the question. Or must I live it all over again, and learn it all over again, in the other forms that belong to the world of men, whose experience yet runs parallel to that of Fairy Land?[19]

Thus ends George MacDonald's first great story. There are many fantastic elements within it that scholars will continue to debate over for many years. Some have leveled improbable claims about Greek mythology and even Mother-Earth symbolism being played out in a fantastic allegory. But while MacDonald used Many Greek and German names, and made allusions to certain ancient tales, it would be foolhardy to try and read very much into this considering he said in a letter to his father that the novel "...took me two months to write without any close work", hardly enough time or effort to concoct all the allegorical themes that many have suggested. And as

MacDonald himself knew only too well, people often see only what they wish to see. He could only hope that his readers would see what they *needed* to see. He refused to elaborate on most of his fictional work, leaving it for the reader to ponder for himself, saying, "Everyone... who feels the story, will read its meaning after his own nature and development: one man will read one meaning in it, another will read another."[20]

He also made a startling self deprecating statement that the meaning an individual may take from one of his stories could well be superior to the one the author intended.

> If he be a true man, he will imagine true things; what matter whether I meant them or not? They are there none the less that I cannot claim putting them there!...in everything God has made, there is layer upon layer of ascending significance; also he expresses the same thought in higher and higher kinds of thought ... A man may well himself discover truth in what he wrote; for he was dealing all the time with things that came from thoughts beyond his own.[21]

Chapter 3
The Life

Today students of George MacDonald's work like to refer to him as a mystic. We like to think of him as, in a special sense, having lived another life in a world away from the material one we find ourselves in at every waking moment. And indeed he took seriously that world of spirit and saw evidence of it in the smallest of everyday occurrences. He believed in the visions of religious rebels like Blake and Swedenborg, and it may be said that at times he believed in them perhaps more than he should have. But, if we desire to classify MacDonald himself with St. John of the Cross or St. Teresa of Avilla we may do ourselves a disservice. MacDonald confessed that he had nothing of the gift of second sight in him, and he mentions no visions or auditory events even though his father, George MacDonald Senior, once said that, as a young boy and later an adolescent, young George had, "longings after visions and revelations." Greville tells us his father had a special faculty for sleep and could lie himself down and doze off almost anywhere in an instant. We'd like to suppose that many of the dream worlds he wrote about came from personal experience. If they did, he seldom made mention of such things. We know that he often took personal experiences from everyday life that happened to himself, his friends, and his family, and infused them into his storylines. We do not know, however, that the dreams, mystical incidents, and otherworldly episodes within his tales, ever happened to him or to those he knew in real life. In fact, he never once granted an interview. The two biographies that his sons, Greville and Ronald, wrote of their famous father mention precious little about any real mystical experiences he may have had. Yet, they refer to their father as having a mystical way about him. Greville records, "There was always a mystical quality in my father's influence: to come within it was to be convinced."[1]

George MacDonald desired "visions and revelations" as a boy, but as a man he had learned, as do all those God speaks to, that these things do not, and will never, come by desire and longing. In fact it's the reverse that seems nearer the truth, and that, in wanting a thing very much, especially spiritual gifts, we will only drive them away. The bible teaches that, "The Spirit of God moves upon him whom he wishes", rather than upon those who desire or expect such giftings. MacDonald learned that *work* is at the center of everything we do, everything we are, and everything we are given.

> But the door into life generally opens behind us, and a hand is put forth which draws us in backwards. The sole wisdom for man or boy who is haunted with the hovering of unseen wings, with the scent of unseen roses, and the subtle enticements of "melodies unheard," is work. If he follow any of those, they will vanish. But if he work, they will come unsought.[2]

Today many people seem to suffer from a great loss of basic language skills, or as Evelyn Underhill once termed it— "verbal bankruptcy". English words are constantly changing, taking on new meanings or dropping out altogether. This is only natural in part, but it is an unhappy state of affairs when we can no longer make ourselves understood. You may recall in the preface to the book you are now reading that we saw how words like: mystic, or mysticism, are often cited by sermonizers today with scorn in their mindset and how they're often linked with occult occurrences and even witchcraft. This is largely due to the ignorance of gothic novelists over the past two centuries along with the mounds of poorly written (and ill-conceived) occult literature that often influenced them. A mystic, or a person who has had a mystical encounter, is simply someone who has been in direct contact with the Divine, whether an angelic messenger, a voice from heaven, a vision, or handwriting appearing on a wall out of nowhere. These things may happen while in or out of the body. But, more often we should associate it with a state in which a person *through no intent of his or her own* will find the bodily senses temporarily dulled and the sense(s) of another existence opened to them in some way. We also mentioned before how St. Paul is frequently cited as the first mystic, or at least as the first mystical writer, with the very mystical text of St. John's Gospel appearing not long after. They suggest the senses of a new world opened to them by way of what Paul refers to as the infilling of the Spirit of God, along with certain powers that seem miraculous in ordinary reality.[3] Now the wise among us will ask themselves how they can know if such incidences are strictly from the Divine rather than from darker corners? After all, don't those students of the dark arts boast of similar occurrences? And, we might add that they also will typically refer to them as "mystical" encounters. But there is one clear differentiating characteristic between the mystic and the follower of occult practices, and MacDonald knew it well. Greville teaches and admonishes us with what his father held true when speaking of Anodos in *Phantastes*:

C.S. LEWIS CALLED HIM MASTER

> ...Anodos steps from his own bed into the daisied grass to see how both Celtic and German poet would have us understand that quite easily and unexpectedly we also may step—*not if we will*, but rather *if we are led*—out of the common tangible world into that truer land of faerie and imagery....[4]

This was something Novalis also taught us, "The striving after the unknown, undetermined is extremely dangerous and disadvantageous. Revelations cannot be forced with force."[5]

The common sorcerer, magician, or witch is one who *seeks out* messages from other worlds and almost always (though they may deny it even to themselves) for selfish purposes. They may seek to learn the future in order to make personal gain by the knowledge it brings, perhaps something as simple as tomorrow's lottery numbers.

The mystic, however, has no *self*, no ambitions, and only desires to be a better person each day. He applies himself to hard work in service to others. And, he seeks only the face of God in his prayers.

We may, nevertheless, have to reluctantly admit that the language has changed during the past 150-years or so, that mystic now means many things to many people, and try to adjust ourselves to the new standard.

G.K. Chesterton, who followed closely on MacDonald's heels, also wrote some tales of such an imaginative magnitude that we could easily conclude there was something of a mystic in him as well. Yet he scarcely mentions anything of a mystical or otherworldly event ever having taken place in his life other than some oddities that occurred while he and brother, Cecil, played with a spirit board as adolescents. In his autobiography he says this about messages from other worlds or spirits:

> My brother and I used to play with planchette, or what the Americans call the ouija board; but we were

among the few, I imagine, who played in a mere spirit of play. Nevertheless I would not altogether rule out the suggestion of some that we were playing with fire; or even with hell-fire. In the words that were written for us there was nothing ostensibly degrading, but any amount that was deceiving. I saw quite enough of the thing to be able to testify, with complete certainty, that something happens which is not in the ordinary sense natural, or produced by the normal and conscious human will. Whether it is produced by some subconscious but still human force, or by some powers, good, bad or indifferent, which are external to humanity, I would not myself attempt to decide. The only thing I will say with complete confidence, about that mystic and invisible power, is that it tells lies. The lies may be larks or they may be lures to the imperiled soul or they may be a thousand other things; but whatever they are, they are not truths about the other world; or for that matter about this world.[6]

One thing we do know of MacDonald was that, although he had many friends, and there were throngs of people always trying to gain an audience with him, like most mystics and metaphysicians he was a loner at heart. He had a great fondness of the sea, of forests, and nature. If the phrase, "alone in a crowd", ever meant anything, it found its fulfillment in George MacDonald. His mind was usually turned inward. And often times it had the effect that it so often has on mystics: that of great sadness. Even as a boy his family had been concerned about his mental state. Regarding his father's depression in his youth, Greville says, "George MacDonald's gaiety of heart was alternated, not only by periods of anxious thought, but often by something akin to despondency. [His older friends were anxious about his spiritual state.]"[7]

C.S. LEWIS CALLED HIM MASTER

From Robert Troop (a friend from school at Aberdeen and later a minister):

> When Maconochie returned about midnight to his sister's, he looked anxious and disturbed, and said: "I hope George Macdonald is not going out of his mind... When we got to the shore, he walked backwards and forwards on the sands amid the howling winds and the beating spray, with the waves coming up to our feet; and all the time he went on addressing the sea and the waves and the storm."[8]

MacDonald did, however, find much solace in his cousin and lifelong friend, Helen MacKay, as Greville again records for us.

> But, fun and high spirits not withstanding, young George MacDonald would have been, I truly think, very lonely, but for this loving friend... She told me also that he was often much depressed ... She said a favorite saying of his then was, "I wis we war a' deid!", [I wish we were all dead!] and that he often repeated it in after life.[9]

Why mystics feel such utter sadness so much of the time is hard to say. It may be that they spend too much time turning inward and too much time trying to ponder mysteries far too great for them. It may be like any one of us being obsessed in trying to imagine the end of forever, knowing in our own good sense that we will never be able to comprehend the incomprehensible, yet not being able to stop ourselves. We wonder why God would allow these people to suffer from such bouts of melancholy, yet the bible is full of examples of prophets who also seem to spend a great deal of their time in utter gloom. It's easy to imagine that we should feel quite happy, even euphoric, after having a vision from God or a visitation from an angel, yet we're told that Daniel was generally troubled in spirit after such events, and that he even suffered illness for several days after at least one vision.

Many of us think that surely God still converses with individuals from time to time in a direct way, like he did with Moses and Abraham. We wonder where is the Moses or the Abraham of today? Then we read a book like *Phantastes* or *The Man Who was Thursday*, and it places such a shudder in our hearts that we feel we've finally found our modern ambassadors of the Almighty, those who walk between two worlds and see visions of splendor that few men see before the grave. Should we suffer disappointment that MacDonald and Chesterton confess they have no such gifts?

It may be that such men as these were as entrenched in the Spirit world as ever any mystic was, but for them it came in a different form. It came in the form of the imagination[10] with words they could scarcely believe they themselves had written at times. MacDonald said it best:

> A fairytale, a sonata, a gathering storm, a limitless night, seizes you and sweeps you away: do you begin at once to wrestle with it and ask whence its power over you, whither it is carrying you?... To one the sonata is a world of odour and beauty, to another of soothing only and sweetness. To one, cloudy rendezvous is a wild dance, with a terror at its heart; to another, a majestic march of heavenly hosts, with Truth in their center pointing their course, but as yet restraining her voice.
>
> ...Does any aspect of Nature awake but one thought?... Is it nothing that she rouses the something deeper than the understanding—the power that underlies thoughts? Does she not set feeling, and so thinking at work?... Nature is mood-engendering,

thought-provoking: such ought the sonata, such ought the fairytale to be.[11]

Ronald MacDonald gives a terrific summary of this quality of the mystical imagination found in his father's words. While speaking of the "passing out" from one world of existence to another within the pages of *Phantastes* and *Lilith*, he says to us:

> In each case, however, the *passing out* thus procured is but a quaint introduction to that country which every man has within himself; though many, it seems, never find it; while of those who do find, most are led to the great discovery by the guiding hand of a poet.
>
> It is the land... of no bargains, where the ego reaches its apotheosis in something better than Nirvana.
>
> From boyhood to old age, I must believe, George MacDonald had the freedom of that country; was fluent and scholarly in its speech as in our own; passed freely, it seems, from it to us, from us to it; but, if one may attempt translating a smatter of its tongue, lived in it most freely while his presence was most vivid among us others. The guidance of pilgrims to this land of faerie, as he loved writing the old word, was his business....
>
> But never did he say the land was of his making; never did he speak of its light as shining more for him or his than for any other man that cometh into the world. He was but one of those who knew the way.
>
> In varying degree every poet, whether of pen, brush, or chisel, gives such guidance. But I am concerned here to show, or, at least, declare, that this one held fast the intent of opening, if it were never so little, the eyes of his fellows to the vision of the unseen;

and to this inflexible continuity of purpose he owed, doubtless, many an adverse contemporary criticism.[12]

George MacDonald would write and find publication for no less than fifty two books during his forty two years as an author. Nearly half of them were novels; the other half consisted of short stories, poetry, sermons, and critical essays. He wrote novels both in the English language and some in his native Scottish tongue. These novels, apart from his fantasies, although they are often criticized today for their overt sermonizing, brought him much attention from the literary world when they were written. His poetry would likewise not be thought of as very grand by today's audiences, except for some of his songs. One particularly nice song was *Faith*:

Faith

"Earth, if aught should check thy race,
Rushing through unfended space,
Headlong, stayless, thou wilt fall
Into yonder glowing ball!"

"Beggar of the universe,
Faithless as an empty purse!
Sent abroad to cool and tame,
Think'st I fear my native flame?"

"If thou never on thy track
Turn thee round and hie thee back,
Thou wilt wander evermore,
Outcast, cold—a comet hoar!"

"While I sweep my ring along
In an air of joyous song,
Thou art drifting, heart awry,

C.S. LEWIS CALLED HIM MASTER

From the sun of liberty!"[13]

Of course it is his fantasies and fairytales that we remember him for best in our day and rightly so. Few authors have ever come close to him in these areas. Whatever drew people to his writing was likely something within the man himself, or more correctly stated: his faith, his gift of wisdom, and his levelheaded approach in all things. That he was a much loved man is hardly an overstatement. He was great friends with Lewis Carroll, John Ruskin, and Mark Twain among other contemporaries. He also befriended the much maligned and very misunderstood Lady Byron, former wife of the famous poet, Lord Byron. While MacDonald wrote an article on Percy Shelley for the Encyclopedia Britannica, Lady Byron supplied him with many insights into the life of Shelley who had been friends with her late husband. She took such a liking to MacDonald's own work as a poet that she became a matron to him throughout much of his life. Though MacDonald's books grew a large international audience, he still found it difficult to support his wife and eleven children on the small income he got from his books and lectures. Lady Byron's support often kept literal starvation from the ever-growing MacDonald family.

Samuel Clemmons (AKA—Mark Twain) had once discussed co-writing a book with MacDonald. Twain was exasperated by the fact that there were no international copyright laws observed by a coalition of countries in those days. While he collected royalties for his books in America, he would get nothing for the sales of those books abroad, especially in England where publishers were doing quite well for themselves selling their own pirated copies of his work. To make matters worse, American publishers seemed unconcerned about this for the simple reason that very few American books ever sold well to other English speaking audiences, these being primarily in the British Isles. Twain, however, was an exception.

GEORGE MACDONALD

Conversely, MacDonald sold well in America and also received no royalties from those sales. Twain's idea seemed inspired enough: two authors from both sides of the Atlantic writing a joint effort might clear the hurdle, with the two men sharing the royalties from both countries between themselves. Unfortunately, the idea was eventually shelved due to stylistic differences. Nevertheless, a great friendship was always maintained. Twain's children were enamored with MacDonald's novel, *At the Back of the North Wind*, written for children but much loved by adults as well. It's still his best selling book.

It may be good to bring to attention here something that Greville said in 1924 before the many biographies appeared on Twain's life. We've seen many of these authors make claims that Twain's religious faith was nearly nonexistent. Some have come very close to making him a champion of atheism. One may get such a notion after reading stories like: *Papers From the Adam Family* or *The Mysterious Stranger* among others. In truth though, Mark Twain was a very spiritual man who wrote about his own doubts in these stories. He doubted much of the bible as literal truth or even as being entirely inspired by God (as did MacDonald which we will see later). Twain might be best described as a searcher who was devoted to truth in religion. Greville says of him:

> So deeply religious a man ... was the great humorist that his father-in-law, Mr. Langdon, had been urgent that he should write a life of Christ, believing that his keen observation and knowledge of men, coupled with his real religious fervour, would startle many into a truer fidelity.[14]

Charles L. Dodgson (AKA—Lewis Carroll) was always a real treat for the MacDonald children to have around. He took them on countless outings. It was these same children to whom he first presented his *Alice in Wonderland* manuscript. They loved it and urged him, along with father George, to try and have it published. He named a white kitten, Snowdrop, in his *Through the Looking-Glass* novel after Mary MacDonald's cat of the same name. Carroll was a fine mathematician, but he was also an avid photographer. He photographed all of the MacDonald children. Because Carroll loved children and often took pictures of them, there were some attempts by onlookers to cast Lewis Carroll as a salacious man who preyed on them. Part of the reason for this outlook was because Carroll sometimes photographed children in the nude. It would appear, however, that these were simply nude studies done in an artistic fashion. The allegations disgusted Carroll to the point of giving up his hobby altogether in 1880. If there were ever any improprieties, the MacDonald children never saw anything of the sort and even as adults they had nothing but admiration for their old friend. But people with minds geared toward lascivious thoughts and desires will often attempt to see those notions fulfilled everywhere they look. One MacDonald biographer once tried to reveal his famous fairytale, *The Light Princess*, as being unseemly because of its ending. A giant snake is used to make a hole in the floor of a lake through which to drain it, but a young man uses his own body to plug the hole, saving the princess in the process. We can be sure that MacDonald would have had a chuckle or two at a biographer's attempt to turn this simple storyline into a sexual allegory. All those who knew George MacDonald would never have believed him capable in the least of doing such a thing (not to mention the fact that the story makes absolutely no sense as a sexual allegory). If he was not as pure as the driven snow it was probably for the simple reason that the snow itself was no match for him.

An unfinished C.S. Lewis manuscript, *The Dark Tower*, underwent the same scrutiny when it was first published several years after his death. One of the characters was a man who had a stinger attached to his forehead by which he would sting people. His poison would then turn them into something resembling a zombie. A biographer with malicious intent endeavored to turn this into a sexual metaphor. More recently a similar attempt was made by a reviewer of Lewis's *The Lion, the Witch and the Wardrobe* after its movie premier. In a scene where a faun (a creature who is part man, part goat) drugs a young girl in order to capture her for a witch who rules the land, it was suggested that there was some "sexual tension" between this little girl and the beast. The suggestion of such a thing left most readers scratching their heads in disbelief at the reviewer. People do indeed see what they want to see. We can only hope the world doesn't take their insinuations as seriously as they themselves so often do.

To say that the MacDonald family was poor would have been an understatement. But, poor or not, the MacDonald's often took in refugees and adopted still more children into their household. In 1872 George MacDonald was made an offer from the famous American lecture bureau—Redpath & Fall, for a tour of the United States. He was forty eight and in poor health but he felt the offer to lecture for eight months abroad at a rate of thirty pounds per lecture, was something he could not ignore. The money was not great; he could indeed have made as much by staying home and writing for the eight months, but the recognition it brought him in the States might bring him more sales in the future, and it would give him a much needed rest from his writing. In September, Mr. and Mrs. George MacDonald along with their fifteen year old son Greville, set course for a twelve day journey to Boston aboard the S.S. Malta. (The S.S. Malta; incidentally, sank off the coast of Cornwall under Kenidjack Castle in 1889 in just ten meters of water and today is a popular spot for divers to visit).

MacDonald lectured primarily on the subjects of Shakespeare (especially *Hamlet*), Tom Hood, Robert Burns, Milton, and Tennyson. The American audiences were very drawn to the poetic works of Burns at this time. The first lecture MacDonald gave in the States happened to be about the famous poet, and these talks in particular brought instant success to the tour. He spoke to crowds of as many as 3,500 from Boston and New York, to Chicago and Montreal. Greville says of the now famous Burns lectures:

> ...without notes or help other than a little volume of Burns's works, he set the man before them ... in true portraiture, while his sins and shortcomings were fully accredited to him. I must have heard him lecture on Burns over forty times, I think, in the States, and used to declare that on every occasion it was a different lecture.[15]

When George MacDonald wasn't lecturing during his time in America, he could often be found preaching in various churches. During his Sunday sermon in Ann Arbor, with the single exception of the Episcopalians, every church in town had shut their doors so that their congregations could go to hear MacDonald preach. The crowds which his sermons drew were nearly as large as those who attended his lectures. He refused, however, to take remittance for these sermons. This infuriated the touring company because, they claimed, why should people pay to see the man lecture when they could go to church and hear him talk for free? It's interesting to note that his son Ronald says concerning his father's preaching that:

> ...his Sundays in many years were filled with preaching from the pulpits of any who might invite him. After his abandonment of the predicant profession, he never took remuneration for a spoken sermon; and never, I am sure, refused his preaching, from whatever Christian denomination the invitation might come.[16]

Money, however, meant very little to George MacDonald. It's also interesting that Ronald MacDonald says that only once did he ever witness his father preaching a sermon that he had written out beforehand, preferring rather to deliver them *ex tempore*. Yet, somewhat ironically, only once does anyone within the MacDonald family ever recall George MacDonald, this man of fantastical imagination, telling a fairytale to one of his children or grandchildren *viva voce*. Not only did he prefer reading to them from a book, but never did he read to them from his own books. Even at public gatherings he would rather read from someone else than from his own work, except occasionally from his poetry and then only quite reluctantly.

During a farewell visit to Boston before sailing home, a dinner was given in his honor. Among the attendees were Oliver Wendell Holmes, Ralph Waldo Emerson, James Fields (editor of the *Atlantic Monthly*) and several other members of the famed Boston Brahmins (a circle of well-known Boston Intellectuals). At this dinner, MacDonald was presented with what was referred to as a *Copyright Testimonial*. American book publishers in those days were nothing short of bandits. He was given $1,500 in recognition of the fact that his books sold in America had paid him practically no compensation. A few days later, while in New York, a group of local deacons came and offered MacDonald $20,000-per-annum to accept a pastorate at their church, an incredible sum of money in those days. He turned it down on the spot, and as Greville suggests, he may have even felt disturbed and offended that such an exorbitant amount was offered for the position.

Much has already been written by others about George MacDonald's childhood on his Father's Scottish farm, most of it fairly uninteresting. His mother died when he was very young, but his stepmother was every bit a real mother to him (he always referred to her as "mother"—never "stepmother"). He remained very close to his parents throughout their lives. There are two incidents concerning his father, George MacDonald Senior, that are worth mentioning.

C.S. LEWIS CALLED HIM MASTER

He had his left leg amputated in 1825, a year after young George was born. This was due to an inflammation of the knee caused by tuberculoses. The doctor who performed the operation told George Junior years later that his father refused alcohol (used as a mild sedative and pain killer in those days), and that, he only flinched once when the knife initially entered the leg. Of course we have to wonder if the doctor wasn't just being kind to young George with those words; however, it became a family legend that was always maintained. His father used a wooden leg thereafter.

Another incident involves the death of George's brother, John Hill MacDonald, at the age of twenty eight. John was perhaps an even more intense thinker than George when it came to metaphysical considerations. His thoughts were often despondent the way George's were in his younger years, but in John's case these thoughts never fully resolved themselves in a belief that God was at the center of things. One of George MacDonald's favorite philosophies revolved around the notion that at the back of every great struggle in spirit and body there is, "one [God] who knows a secret too great to tell." John had difficulty accepting this. To him the universe was often a dreadful thing to contemplate. But he always had a hope that existence was not for nothing. His depression seemed to stem from the fact that he could see no reason to think that any earthly thing, nor the universe itself, had any real existence other than in the mind. In this he was uncertain however, and struggled with the thought of it all. (Perhaps this later inspired his brother, George, to write in *Unspoken Sermons* that, "We must not wonder things away into nonentity.")[17] Mystics often see the world in just this way, but they see the mind of God at the back of it all and this satisfies them. John was not so easily assured. Even if all existed in thought alone, he could not be sure that it was God's thought. But the hope eternal was always there as he shows in a letter to his brother George two years before his death:

48

GEORGE MACDONALD

...I seem to myself at times like a curiously contrived machine exquisitely adjusted up to a certain point—where the Maker seems suddenly to have relaxed his efforts and given so hurried a finishing touch as to spoil it for going to all coming time. But I know this figure will not please you, who prefer to consider the mind itself as the creator and upholder of the organism. [George MacDonald certainly thought like a mystic along these lines]. This much, however is now plain to me, that life can only be measured by a series of activities [events], and that for those who cannot realize existence at all except under some form of beauty and loftiness, life ceases when these activities do not tend to the productions of these conceptions. And here I think is the true province of faith which assures us that these things do in fact exist, although we can only come temporarily in contact with them—yea, that nothing else can be truly said to exist at all, however it may possess a temporary and transitory existence, except what is great and worth living for. This assured conviction must be the faith of which Christ speaks when he will be in a man as a well of water springing up into everlasting life.[18]

It is indeed a very mystical outlook on the words of Christ that John offers us.

Only a few days after John MacDonald's death, George MacDonald Senior was going out a gate that led from the farm to a back road when he spotted a man coming toward the gate. The man passed him and then turned, and when he did, the father recognized him as his recently deceased son. He tried to follow after him (bear in mind that he had a wooden leg by this time) around the bend to a large open clearing but couldn't see him anywhere even though there was no place to hide. He took it as a sign that his son's ghost was giving him a message that he would soon be following him in death. George MacDonald Senior did in fact die just a few weeks later of a sudden heart attack.

Chapter 4
The Un-Fundamentalist

To talk in depth about George MacDonald's particular religious affiliations would be pointless. He was raised a Congregationalist and later in life became an Anglican, but sects were not important to him as such. His was not a God of factions or even necessarily of religion as most of us know it. His God was one that revealed himself in different ways to different people. This revealed God might come through reflection in holy writings often enough; to MacDonald, the bible was not about man's search for God but about God's revelation to man. The bible however, was something that only brought you to a certain precipice. From there the deeper reflection of the individual's soul took the helm.

> There are thoughts and feelings that cannot be called up in the mind by any power of will or force of imagination; which, being spiritual, must arise in the soul when in its highest spiritual condition; when the mind, indeed, like a smooth lake, reflects only heavenly images....[1]

C.S. LEWIS CALLED HIM MASTER

He saw God's thoughts at work in everything that surrounded man. MacDonald could almost be called a naturalist, but his was not the naturalism of the pantheist. Yet nature was very inspiring to him; he had an unusual affinity for the sea, for mountains, trees, and flowers, even oddly enough — for gems — their multifaceted reflection of light and color was a suggestion of multidimensional heaven itself all around us if we could but see it with spiritual eyes.

All of life, whether waking or asleep, held a lesson to be learned. And, if we would remain obstinate to the end and not learn what we must, then hell itself would push us and humble us into rightness. But George MacDonald's God was not a God of *eternal* tortures. He thought that if hell existed at all, it was probably only a temporary state that brought about repentance — a refining fire. He had studied Greek texts all his life and knew full well that the concept of a fiery place of torment was an invention of the Greeks which the Jews likely picked up while in Roman captivity. There was no hell in the Old Testament, just the typical dark, shadowy underworlds that had been so manifest in the texts of all the people from the Mesopotamian area since the ancient Sumerians first wrote of them. But, once the Jews found themselves living among the Romans, they had suddenly picked up more than a few Roman traits in their ideas. Only a few books in the New Testament mention hell, particularly the Gospel of Mathew. The Gospel of John makes no mention of hell nor of eternal tortures of any kind. And, MacDonald was well aware of the many problems in the text of Mathew: the genealogies that seemed quite at odds with those found in Luke's gospel, the many quotes from Old Testament books that were said to be prophetic of Jesus but of which there didn't seem to be any clear connection. A great example would of course be Mathew's use of Isaiah 7:14 to support a virgin birth for Christ, however, a closer inspection of Isaiah 7:14 and the next few chapters seems rather to be a narrative about the birth of a son (Maher-Shalal-Hash-Baz) that was born to Isaiah himself and a prophetess as a sign for a king to go to war.

We don't know what MacDonald thought about the reliability of the virgin birth story. We can only conjecture about his position as to whether or not it was a trustworthy account. However, to believe or disbelieve in the virgin birth is one thing, but that creeds and doctrines would later contain phrasing based on something as fragile as the virgin birth accounts would be the type of sloppy thinking in the church that brought out the Holy wrath of George MacDonald.[2]

The scholar in MacDonald would question any biblical passage that he felt would cast God in an unsavory light or that didn't stand to reason—how could he not and keep his integrity? It was more than mere scholarship and philosophy that caused him to question the concept of eternal torture however; his God-given conscience travailed at the very thought of such a state for any soul to be in.

> Primarily, God is not bound to punish sin; he is bound to destroy sin....
>
> Punishment, I repeat, is not the thing required of God, but the absolute destruction of sin. What better is the world, what better is the sinner, what better is God, what better is the truth, that the sinner should suffer—continue suffering to all eternity? Would there be less sin in the universe? Would there be any making-up for sin? Would it show God justified in doing what he knew would bring sin into the world, justified in making creatures who he knew would sin? What setting-right would come of the sinner's suffering? If justice demand it, if suffering be the equivalent for sin, then the sinner must suffer, then God is bound to exact his suffering, and not pardon; and so the making of man was a tyrannical deed, a creative cruelty. But grant that the

sinner has deserved to suffer, no amount of suffering is any atonement for his sin. To suffer to all eternity could not make up for one unjust word. Does that mean, then, that for an unjust word I deserve to suffer to all eternity? The unjust word is an eternally evil thing; nothing but God in my heart can cleanse me from the evil that uttered it; but does it follow that I saw the evil of what I did so perfectly, that eternal punishment for it would be just? Sorrow and confession and self-abasing love will make up for the evil word; suffering will not. For evil in the abstract, nothing can be done. It is eternally evil. But I may be saved from it by learning to loathe it, to hate it, to shrink from it with an eternal avoidance. The only vengeance worth having on sin is to make the sinner himself its executioner. Sin and punishment are in no antagonism to each other in man, any more than pardon and punishment are in God; they can perfectly co-exist. The one naturally follows the other, punishment being born of sin, because evil exists only by the life of good, and has no life of its own, being in itself death. Sin and suffering are not natural opposites; the opposite of evil is good, not suffering; the opposite of sin is not suffering, but righteousness. The path across the gulf that divides right from wrong is not the fire, but repentance. If my friend has wronged me, will it console me to see him punished? Will that be a rendering to me of my due? Will his agony be a balm to my deep wound? Should I be fit for any friendship if that were possible even in regard to my enemy? But would not the shadow of repentant grief, the light of reviving love on his countenance, heal it at once however deep? Take any of those wicked people in Dante's hell, and ask wherein is justice served by their punishment. Mind, I am not saying it is not right to punish them; I am saying that justice is not, never can be, satisfied by suffering—nay, cannot have any satisfaction in or from suffering. Human resentment, human revenge, human hate may. Such justice as Dante's keeps wickedness alive in its most terrible forms. The life of God goes forth to inform, or at least give a home to victorious evil. Is he not defeated every time that one of those lost souls defies him? All hell cannot make Vanni Fucci say 'I was wrong.' God is triumphantly defeated, I say, throughout the hell of his vengeance. Although against evil, it is but the vain and wasted cruelty of a tyrant. There is no destruction of evil thereby, but an enhancing of its horrible power in the midst of the most agonizing and disgusting tortures a divine imagination can invent. If sin must be kept alive, then hell must be kept alive; but while I regard the smallest sin as infinitely loathsome, I do not believe that any being, never good enough to see the essential ugliness of sin, could sin so as to deserve such punishment. I am not now, however, dealing with the question of the duration of punishment, but with the idea of punishment itself; and would only say in passing, that the notion that a creature born imperfect, nay, born with impulses to evil not of his own generating, and which he could not help having, a creature to whom the true face of God was never presented, and by whom it never could have been seen, should be thus condemned, is as loathsome a lie against God as could find place in heart too undeveloped to understand what justice is, and too low to look up into the face of Jesus. It never in truth found place in any heart, though in many a pettifogging brain. There is but one thing lower than deliberately to believe such a lie, and that is to worship the God of whom it is believed. The one deepest, highest, truest, fittest, most wholesome suffering must be generated in the wicked by a vision, a true sight, more or less adequate, of the hideousness of their lives, of the horror of the wrongs they have done. Physical suffering may be a factor in rousing this mental pain; but 'I would I had never been born!' must be the cry of Judas, not because of the hell-fire around him, but because he loathes the man that betrayed his friend, the world's friend. When a man loathes himself, he has begun to be saved. Punishment tends to this result. Not for its own sake, not as a make-up for sin, not for divine revenge—horrible word, not for any satisfaction to justice, can punishment exist. Punishment is for the sake of amendment and atonement. God is bound by his love to punish sin in order to deliver his creature; he is bound by his justice to destroy sin in his creation. Love is justice—is the fulfilling of the law, for God as well as for his children. This is the reason of punishment; this is why justice requires that the wicked shall not go unpunished—that they, through the eye-opening power of pain, may come to see and do justice, may be brought to desire and make all possible amends, and so become just. Such punishment concerns justice in the deepest degree. For Justice, that is God, is bound in himself to see justice done by his children—not in the mere outward act, but in their very being. He is bound in himself to make up for wrong done by his children, and he can do nothing to make up for wrong done but by bringing about the repentance of the wrong-doer. When the man says, 'I did wrong; I hate myself and my deed; I cannot endure to think that I did it!' then, I say, is atonement begun. Without that, all that the Lord did would be lost. He would have made no atonement. Repentance, restitution, confession, prayer for forgiveness, righteous dealing thereafter, is the sole possible, the only true make-up for sin. For nothing less than this did Christ die. When a man acknowledges the right he denied before; when he says to the wrong, "I abjure, I loathe you; I see now what you are; I could not see it before because I would not; God forgive me; make me clean, or let me die!" then justice, that is God, has conquered-and not till then.

....

The notion that the salvation of Jesus is a salvation from the consequences of our sins, is a false, mean, low notion. The salvation of Christ is salvation from the smallest tendency or leaning to sin. It is a deliverance into the pure air of God's ways of thinking and feeling. It is a salvation that makes the heart pure, with the will and choice of the heart to be pure. To such a heart, sin is disgusting. It sees a thing as it is,—that is, as God sees it, for God sees everything as it is. The soul thus saved would rather sink into the flames of hell than steal into heaven and skulk there under the shadow of an imputed righteousness. No soul is saved that would not prefer hell to sin. Jesus did not die to save us from punishment; he was called Jesus because he should save his people from their sins.[3]

Of course many people accused George MacDonald of Universalism because of his stance on hell; however, it wasn't that MacDonald thought there couldn't be a hell, but rather, that *if* there was such a state, either no one would go there or that they wouldn't stay there long if they did.

George MacDonald was no fundamentalist; he felt the weight of no obligation toward the worship of a book, not even the bible, as did (and do) so many others claiming to belong to Christ. He saw as a young boy in Scotland, under the strict code of Calvinism, the dangers that arose in doing so. Greville speaking of his father's studies at Highbury (a theology school) says:

But likely enough, his studies were of other importance than the professors presumed: they were strengthening his suspicions already germinating, that mere scholarship in the interpretation of Christ's words was of small worth, if not often dangerous; though almost up to his last days he was searching his Greek Testament for its innermost meanings.[4]

Eternal torture was hardly the only teaching that MacDonald rebelled against during his Calvinist upbringing. Something that troubled him just as deeply was their stance on predestination. John Calvin's philosophy of double predestination went something like this, "We call predestination God's eternal decree, by which he determined within himself what he willed to become of each man. For all are not created in equal condition; rather, eternal life is foreordained for some, eternal damnation for others."[5]

Single predestination is the less severe form of the teaching. Some Christians have asserted that their relationship to God depends only on God and on God's eternal decree established before the foundation of the world. This point of view is implied only twice in the New Testament: in Ephesians 1, and especially in Romans 8:

> "For those whom he foreknew he also predestined to be conformed to the image of his Son... And those whom he predestined he also called; and those whom he called he also justified; and those whom he justified he also glorified." (Romans 8:29-30)

These verses imply single predestination, because they concern only predestination to life with God and say nothing about a hellish damnation.

GEORGE MACDONALD

George MacDonald would write of the subject many years later, "I well remember feeling as a child that I did not care for God to love me if he did not love everybody."[6]

MacDonald was undoubtedly part of the great rebellion towards the stricter tenants of Calvinism during the middle part of 19th century Scotland. Greville tells us his father would have indeed been considered by some (including his brother Charles) as being one of many "black sheep" at the Blackfriar's Congregational Church in Aberdeen, a group of mostly young men who simply could see no sense in much of what they saw in Calvinist teaching.

And although he hated the rigors of *learning* the Shorter Catechism as a boy, it was its *teaching* he came to loath as a man. The opening line goes, "The chief end of man is to glorify God and enjoy him forever." MacDonald would later respond to this, "For my part, I wish the spiritual engineers who constructed it had, after laying the grandest foundation-stone that truth could afford them, glorified God by going no further."[7]

Fortunately for young George, his father had similar reservations concerning Calvinism. George MacDonald Senior would write to his son in 1850:

> Like you, I cannot by any means give in to the extreme points either of Calvinism or Arminianism, nor can I bear to see that which is evidently gospel mystery torn to pieces by those who believe there is no mystery in the scriptures and therefore attempt to explain away what is evidently for the honor of God to conceal. I see so much of mystery in nature, and so much of it in myself, that it would be a proof to my mind that the scriptures were not from God were there nothing in them beyond the grasp of my own mind.[8]

Critical Biblical scholarship was already in full bloom by the time MacDonald was a boy during the first half of the 19th century. The Pentateuch had by this time been dissected into the now commonplace J, P, E, and D writers rather than the previously absurd notion that Moses had written it all himself. (In order to have pulled this off Moses would have had to have written about his own death, refer to himself as the most humble man on the face of the Earth, compare himself with the prophets who came after him, and give brief accounts of kings and kingdoms that didn't exist until long after he was dead). MacDonald was friends with Oxford biblical scholar, Dean Stanley, and together they had no doubt kept a watchful eye on the work of fellow scholars in the field such as Graf, Vatke and the incomparable Julius Wellhausen. Still, then as now, the "powers that be" which were at the center of church dominance in greater Christendom, were generally unwilling to allow that they and the church fathers had at times been wrong in their thinking and teaching even under the microscope of honest scholarship. MacDonald might have suggested to them that, "A lie for God is a lie against God."

George MacDonald's deepest convictions concerning the bible, biblical inspiration, and what it takes to truly be a Christian were probably best summed up in a letter he wrote to an unidentified woman that had written him (apparently expressing disapproval), asking why he had left so much of the old faith behind. It may be the most important document ever written against the core of Christian fundamentalist teaching—biblical infallibility.

Have you really been reading my books, and at this time ask me what have I lost of the old faith? Much have I rejected of the new, but I have never rejected anything I could keep, and have never turned to gather again what I had once cast away. With the faith itself to be found in the old Scottish manse I trust I have a true sympathy. With many of the forms gathered around that faith and supposed by the faithful to set forth and explain their faith, I have none. At a very early age I had begun to cast them from me; but all the time my faith in Jesus as the Son of the Father of men and the Savior of us all, has been growing. If it were not for the fear of its sounding unkind, I would say that if you had been a disciple of his instead of mine, you would not have mistaken me so much. Do not suppose that I believe in Jesus because it is said so-and-so in a book. I believe in him because he is himself. The vision of him in that book, and, I trust, his own living power in me, have enabled me to understand him, to look him in the face, as it were, and accept him as my Master and Savior, in following whom I shall come to the rest of the Father's peace. The Bible is to me the most precious thing in the world, because it tells me his story; and what good men thought about him who know him and accepted him. But, the common theory of the inspiration of the words, instead of the breathing of God's truth into the hearts and souls of those who wrote it, and who then did their best with it, is degrading and evil; and they who hold it are in danger of worshipping the letter instead of living in the Spirit, of being idolaters of the Bible instead of disciples of Jesus.... It is Jesus who is the Revelation of God, not the Bible; that is but a means to a mighty eternal end. The book is indeed sent us by God, but it nowhere claims to be His very word. If it were—and it would be no irreverence to say it—it would have been a good deal better written. Yet even its errors and blunders do not touch the truth, and are the merest trifles—dear as the little spot of earth on the whiteness of the snowdrop. Jesus alone is The Word of God.

With all sorts of doubt I am familiar, and the result of them is, has been, and will be, a widening of my heart and soul and mind to greater glories of the truth—the truth that is in Jesus—and not in Calvin or

Luther or St. Paul or St. John, save as they got it from Him, from whom every simple heart may have it, and can alone get it. You cannot have such proof of the existence of God or the truth of the Gospel story as you can have of a proposition in Euclid or a chemical experiment. But the man who will order his way by the word of the Master shall partake of his peace, and shall have in himself a growing conviction that in him are hid all the treasures of wisdom and knowledge....

One thing more I must say: though the Bible contains many an utterance of the will of God, we do not need to go there to find how to begin to do his will. In every heart there is a consciousness of some duty or other required of it: that is the will of God. He who would be saved must get up and do that will—if it be but to sweep a room or make an apology, or pay a debt. It was he who had kept the commandments whom Jesus invited to be his follower in poverty and labour....

From your letter it seems that to be assured of my faith would be a help to you. I cannot say I never doubt, nor until I hold the very heart of good as my very own in Him, can I wish not to doubt. For doubt is the hammer that breaks the windows clouded with human fancies, and lets in the pure light. But I do say that all my hope, all my joy, all my strength are in the Lord Christ and his Father; that all my theories of life and growth are rooted in him; that his truth is gradually clearing up the mysteries of this world.... To Him I belong heart and soul and body, and he may do with me as he will—nay, nay—I pray him to do with me as he wills: for that is my only well-being and freedom.[9]

Two last notes about the man's faith are needed. While he rebelled from an early age toward Calvinism and certain other doctrines he found hard to follow, he had an absolute abhorrence of schism and sects. This is very clear from much of his writing. Even during the great schism that split the Congregationalist Church during the 1840's and created the Free Church, and even considering MacDonald's sympathies in doctrinal disputes toward those who felt it necessary to leave the church, he himself never left it until much later in life, and then, for unknown reasons—he left it quietly and turned to the Church of England.

And lastly, while MacDonald could never hold to a doctrine of biblical infallibility given his integrity, he would always fear the possible consequences that would come when others finally accepted this same view, as surely there would be many who would be only too happy to pick and choose from the bible those things which would suit their selfish desires. But, haven't people always done this anyway— unselfconsciously? He knew how easily people were led by their own egocentric cravings and ambitions. Even during his Calvinistic rebellion this was something that would burden him, as his son Ronald tells us:

> ...He was at one time known most widely for his fight against the Calvinistic doctrines of election and eternity of punishment. Today, I think he might be pained to see how base a sense of freedom from obligation has arisen as a byproduct of a religious movement in which he took so influential a part.[10]

George MacDonald - 1855   Louisa MacDonald - Date Unknown

George, Louisa, All Eleven MacDonald Children, and
Mary MacDonald's Fiancé--Edward Hughes (Back Row, Far Right)

GEORGE MACDONALD

George MacDonald - 1880

Louisa MacDonald - 1885

Louisa With Lewis Carroll & Four of the MacDonald Children - 1862

C.S. LEWIS CALLED HIM MASTER

Back: George MacDonald, J.A. Froude, Wilkie Collins, Anthony Trollope
Front: W.M. Thackeray, Lord Macaulay, Bulwer Lytton, Thomas Carlyle, Charles Dickens

George MacDonald - 1884
In Pilgrim's Progress Play

George and Louisa at Their Golden Wedding Anniversary - 1901

All Photos by Lewis Carroll

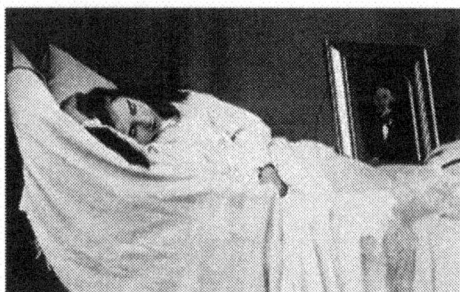

George With Lily - 1863

Mary Josephine MacDonald

Flora Rankin - 1863
Fostered by the MacDonalds

Lilia Scott MacDonald as
Christiana In Pilgrim's Progress Play

Nelly MacDonald

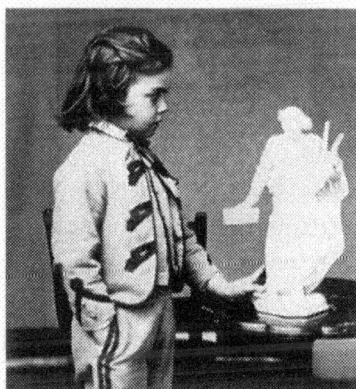

Greville MacDonald

Chapter 5
Lilith

ilith was the second to last book MacDonald wrote, and its often rated by readers as his masterpiece. His son Greville referred to it as "The Revelation of St. George", partly because of how quickly and effortlessly he wrote the original version, so quick in fact that it appeared to those watching him as though he were channeling the very thoughts of God, but also because of the nature of the book. Now from the very start we have to consider this comment. You may remember in our discussion of *Phantastes* that George MacDonald wrote in a letter to his father that it, "...took me two months to write without any close work." We also know from Greville's biography that his father enjoyed writing fantasy stories quite a bit, but they didn't sell well like his novels did, so he mostly stuck to writing novels when it came to fiction. We might construe from this that fantasy came easy for George MacDonald and that this was the reason he wrote *Lilith* so quickly, as well as *Phantastes*. Unlike *Phantastes* though, he did several rewrites of *Lilith* before finally publishing it.

GEORGE MACDONALD

The opening lengthy quotation from the latter half of Henry David Thoreau's beautiful prose piece, "Walking", an essay from his book, *Excursions*, actually gives away the entire premise of the novel, although we shouldn't be surprised at it.

I took a walk on Spaulding's Farm the other afternoon. I saw the setting sun lighting up the opposite side of a stately pine wood. Its golden rays straggled into the aisles of the wood as into some noble hall. I was impressed as if some ancient and altogether admirable and shining family had settled there in that part of the land called Concord, unknown to me,—to whom the sun was servant,—who had not gone into society in the village,—who had not been called on. I saw their park, their pleasure-ground, beyond through the wood, in Spaulding's cranberry meadow. The pines furnished them with gables as they grew. Their house was not obvious to vision; their trees grew through it. I do not know whether I heard the sounds of a suppressed hilarity or not. They seemed to recline on the sunbeams. They have sons and daughters. They are quite well. The farmer's cart-path, which leads directly through their hall, does not in the least put them out,—as the muddy bottom of a pool is sometimes seen through the reflected skies. They never heard of Spaulding, and do not know that he is their neighbor,—notwithstanding I heard him whistle as he drove his team through the house. Nothing can equal the serenity of their lives. Their coat of arms is simply a lichen. I saw it painted on the pines and oaks. Their attics were in the tops of the trees. They are of no politics. There was no noise of labor. I did not perceive that they were weaving or spinning. Yet I did detect, when the wind lulled and hearing was done away, the finest imaginable sweet musical hum,—as of a distant hive in May, which perchance was the sound of their thinking. They had no idle thoughts, and no one without could see their work, for their industry was not as in knots and excrescences embayed.

But I find it difficult to remember them. They fade irrevocably out of my mind even now while I speak and endeavor to recall them, and recollect myself. It is only after a long and serious effort to recollect my best thoughts that I become again aware of their cohabitancy. If it were not for such families as this, I think I should move out of Concord.

The premise of course being the interaction between different worlds. While MacDonald used the land of fairy as a symbol of the spiritual world in many stories prior, here it's quite different. In this story we find talk of multi-dimensional space and time, and no mention of fairyland. Unlike *Phantastes*, this novel is not subtitled "A Faerie Romance", it's simply called, "A Romance", and rightly so. He wants us to *believe* in this other world as he himself felt it and breathed its essence throughout his life. And yet there are fantastical elements sprinkled throughout *Lilith*—a talking raven that is also a man, people that turn into leopards, a vampire-lady, miniature animals ala *Gulliver's Travels*, and much more.

Lilith was first written in 1890 and then rewritten at least four times before its published draft in 1895. The five main versions (there were three others that had only small grammatical errors corrected) were made available through Johannesen Publishing in the 1990's. In 1994 the original 1st version was published together with the final 5th draft in a single volume. Then in 1997 the 2nd, 3rd, 4th, and 5th drafts were all published in a two volume set (*Lilith*—A VARIORUM EDITION) edited by Rolland Hein. They're an interesting read (although some readers will undoubtedly wish they had access to the multitude of marginal notes that would have been difficult to publish for various reasons), but here we will deal only with the final draft that most of us are familiar with.

Einstein said that anyone who says they understand time is a liar. We might say the same of anyone who says that they completely comprehend all the elements that make up *Lilith*. What we can say with certainty is that *Lilith* is not only the most complex fictional work given to us by MacDonald but it is also the most overtly Christian of his fantasy literature. When Mr. Vane, Lona, and the "little ones" ascend to "The City", we are told in plain English that this is Heaven and that some of the beings there are angels. The Christian pilgrimage is plain to see throughout the book. Yet, at the same time there are more fantastical components to be deciphered in *Lilith* than in any other of MacDonald's tales.

In the book's opening we find a young Mr. Vane who has just concluded his education at Oxford, whose parents had died while he was just a boy, and he, being their only child, has now inherited their estate, a house with a great library (how those libraries *do* keep showing up in MacDonald's stories!) which occupies most of the ground floor of this large estate. Mr. Vane seems to be examining his new inheritance as though he has never seen it before even though it belonged to his parents and his grandparents before them and on back for several generations. We later learn that he was taken away by a guardian after his parent's death and has never been back to the house until now, and he is, "...nearly as much alone in the world as a man might find himself". He spends most of his time in the library reading, so much so, that very little of the rest of the house is ever described to us although it is a large estate with servants.

One day he sees a perplexing sight, the figure of a tall man reaching for a book, but then the man quickly seems to disappear, and Mr. Vane concludes that his eyes must have been playing him a trick. This ghostly figure of an old stooped man reappears twice over the course of about a month, and eventually Mr. Vane follows after him as the old man navigates his way through the mansion. After coming to a garret on the second floor the old gentleman once again disappears, and here the young man finds something that will change his whole outlook on existence. What he finds is a small room within the garret which contains at least two mirrors. The room itself revolves at the pulling of a chain and a sliver of light is let in through the roof-hood. Eventually we learn that these mirrors, when properly aligned, will reflect the image of another world, and that, a man may find physical passage through one of the mirrors at this time into that world. There is nothing of the imaginative world of fairy in this account, but rather, the talk of speculative physical science and multiple dimensions. Even someone with a materialist outlook may read these passages and think to himself that this could really happen, that this is not so different from the various "many worlds theories" which theoretical physicists have talked about for many years. This may well be one of the goals MacDonald had in mind while writing his story—to show the spirit world as an actuality—or at least to conjure the possibility of such a world to the mind of a materialist.

Mr. Vane goes to the world beyond the glass on four different occasions. There would seem a fifth toward the end of the book except that he had only dreamed of being back home while he was really still in the other world. The old man says he is a sexton and leads Mr. Vane to his home, in the back of which is a room so large that it is seemingly without walls, a room where the sleeping dead lie, and have lain, some for many generations, waiting to come awake, or "truly awake" as the sexton would say.[1] The sexton (Mr. Raven) and his wife as it turns out are Adam and Eve, the first man and the first woman. But the story takes a turn from a legend found in the Kabala which claims that Adam had a wife before Eve whose name was Lilith. According to MacDonald's new take on the legend, Lilith gave herself to evil and removed herself from Adam's presence.

Then God gave Eve to Adam. Readers should take note here that MacDonald was no great admirer of Jewish Mysticism and probably thought very little importance in the legend of Lilith. So little in fact that he completely rewrote it to his own use and liking. But he did find an inkling of an idea in the notion of Adam having another wife prior to Eve who was evil and in league with the Devil. He took this basic notion and extended it further, wondering, what would it be like if Lilith could be redeemed? This same Lilith who (according to our story) had been at the side of Satan almost since the dawn of mankind helping to aid in the destruction of their souls! Like most of MacDonald's books, this is a story of redemption, the redemption of Lilith, of Mr. Vane, and all those he meets along the way. It is no less than the redemption of the whole world in the end, where all of those who are dead in sin shall finally awake to life after sleeping in the sexton's (Adam's) cemetery where they live in dream after dream, growing in the knowledge of who they truly are and in Whose imagination they truly live and move and have their being.

There is also at least one story about Lilith from Jewish folklore which says that Lilith and her demonic cohorts hide in the corners of mirrors, waiting to enter those who gaze into the looking glass with vanity in their hearts. This is likely where MacDonald came up with the idea of using a mirror to enter this other world where Lilith is the Queen of a wicked city, rather than being influenced by Lewis Carroll's *Alice* books as many have suggested. Actually, Carroll was much more influenced by MacDonald. He wrote *Alice in Wonderland* within four years of the publication of *Phantastes*. That *Phantastes* played a large part in the germination of ideas that ended in the *Alice* books is almost without question. We of course know that Carroll first gave MacDonald *Alice In Wonderland* to read for his approval before attempting to have it published, and we also know Carroll had in his possession a copy of *Phantastes* when he died. As of this writing, Carroll's personal copy of *Phantastes* (which is signed CL Dodgson on the title page) is for sale by a book collector in the UK with an estimated value of nearly $13,000-dollars.

To add to this cast we find that Adam and Lilith once had a child together named Lona, who would become Mr. Vane's own love interest, and also we find that Adam and Eve have a daughter, Mara, who helps her parents in their work with the dead. The other children of Adam mentioned in the bible are not found in this tale. Why is hard to say, but we must remember that, like many of the biblical stories, MacDonald's are also there for the purpose of teaching moral truths more than they are for the sake of teaching a history lesson. *Lilith* is almost entirely didactic (moralistic) in nature, and it is probably for this reason that it was not well received in 1895. Everybody likes being well—nobody likes taking medicine.

There are several curious incidents in *Lilith*, things said or done by characters, that make us wonder why they are even in the story, or what, if any, deeper meaning they may have had in MacDonald's mind for having written them. A good example is in the paper that was written by Mr. Vane's father, which his son finds in a hidden closet within the library. His father writes of his own meeting with Mr. Raven, and on this occasion the sexton tells a little bit about himself and how he (remembering this is Adam himself) had been the librarian for Sir Upward, one of the early ancestors to whom this mansion belonged and of whose likeness there hangs a painting in the library. Now the curious thing for us is that, although Mr. Raven (Adam) has been alive for thousands of years and once walked and talked with God in a garden that was for all intents—another world— he stills says this of Sir Upward as the paper records:

> "You knew my father, then, I presume?" [Mr. Vane's father speaking to Mr. Raven]
> "I knew him," he answered with a curious smile, "but he did not care about my acquaintance, and we

never met.—That gentleman, however," he added, pointing to the portrait,—"old Sir Up'ard, his people called him,—was in his day a friend of mine yet more intimate than ever your grandfather became."

Then at length I began to think the interview a strange one. But in truth it was hardly stranger that my visitor should remember Sir Upward, than that he should have been my great-grandfather's librarian!

"I owe him much," he continued; "for, although I had read many more books than he, yet, through the special direction of his studies, he was able to inform me of a certain relation of modes which I should never have discovered of myself, and could hardly have learned from any one else."

"Would you mind telling me all about that?" I said.

'By no means—as much at least as I am able: there are not such things as willful secrets," he answered—and went on.

"That closet held his library—a hundred manuscripts or so, for printing was not then invented. One morning I sat there, working at a catalogue of them, when he looked in at the door, and said, 'Come.' I laid down my pen and followed him—across the great hall, down a steep rough descent, and along an underground passage to a tower he had lately built, consisting of a stair and a room at the top of it. The door of this room had a tremendous lock, which he undid with the smallest key I ever saw. I had scarcely crossed the threshold after him, when, to my eyes, he began to dwindle, and grew less and less. All at once my vision seemed to come right and I saw that he was moving swiftly away from me. In a minute more he was the merest speck in the distance, with the tops of blue mountains beyond him, clear against a sky of paler blue.

I recognized the country, for I had gone there and come again many a time, although I had never known this way to it.

"Many years after, when the tower had long disappeared, I taught one of his descendants what Sir Upward had taught me; and now and then to this day I use your house when I want to go the nearest way home. I must indeed—without your leave, for which I ask your pardon—have by this time well established a right of way through it—not from front to back, but from bottom to top!"

"You would have me then understand, Mr. Raven," I said, "that you go through my house into another world, heedless of disparting space?"

"That I go through it is an incontrovertible acknowledgment of space," returned the old librarian.

"Please do not quibble, Mr. Raven," I rejoined. "Please to take my question as you know I mean it."

"There is in your house a door, one step through which carries me into a world very much another than this."

"A better?"

"Not throughout; but so much another that most of its physical, and many of its mental laws are different from those of this world. As for moral laws, they must everywhere be fundamentally the same."[2]

This is very curious indeed. Adam is the great teacher throughout MacDonald's tale; teaching morality to the wayward is in fact the whole of God's purpose for Adam, Eve, and Mara. This is the work they are in the world to do. But, while Adam is a teacher of morality (he and Eve having worked their way back into God's good graces many years earlier), he apparently knows very little of science or metaphysics, nor of how God's two (or more) worlds work together. He claims there are at least seven dimensions and ten senses when the spirit and the material worlds are combined, yet he knows almost nothing of time, space, and dimensions, or how these things work in conjunction. What little he knows of them he has learned from a well-read man (Sir Upward) born long after him, who had in turn studied from others. Many readers will undoubtedly wonder why God has told Adam so little about His worlds and why there are others who know so much? We never do find the answer to this mystery. And this is only one of several curious storylines that seem to mean little to the novel, or to MacDonald's morality teaching within it, and of which we are given no answer by the book's end. Yet, they are details that keep us intrigued long after the book's finish. But life is full of questions like these that have always puzzled man. We may look into the night sky and wonder what the point is in the universe being as large as it is? Why billions of stars? Wouldn't a few thousand have worked just as well? Some theologians have suggested that God created man because he was lonely. But, why then are there billions of people on this planet? How many friends does God need?, (if in fact he needed any humans for friendship at all, which seems unlikely to many of us). A child might ask what purpose is there for wings on an ostrich or why people have two small nostrils instead of one large one? There are many, many things in creation that seem to be created without purpose. It may make us wonder at times if God was the creator behind all of them or only some of them? It almost seems as though the world runs on a sort of autopilot much of the time, as though God set the stage, the props, and the actors into position, and then gave up the director's chair to another. And, this other director disassembled some of those props and used the materials to make new kinds of props that were never meant to be in the cosmic script to begin with and which make no sense to the story. And, this new director keeps secrets— secrets which he only tells to a few insiders. But, God has secrets of his own, and his secrets are greater. They are what

C.S. LEWIS CALLED HIM MASTER

MacDonald means when he says over and over in his tales that, through times of adversity and loneliness we should try to remember that, there is a greater good coming than we can now know. Whether MacDonald inserted details into his stories that seemed at odds with normality as a way of showing the unpredictable nature of the world, or of God himself, or whether he sometimes simply wrote whatever came into his head without questioning it, thinking that it had a certain indefinable *something* in it that might be worth sharing with others, is hard to say.

Before we venture farther into *Lilith*, it might do us good to remember that many of the people/beings in the story take on more than one identity, and this is likely to be one of the more confusing elements in the novel for many people reading it for the first time. It may take several readings before things become clear. For example: Mr. Raven, Adam, the sexton, and the old librarian are all the same person. He started his life as Adam in the Garden of Eden and then thousands of years later, for some reason unknown to us, he became the librarian for one of Mr. Vane's ancestors (Sir Upward was probably the first). Why Adam is suddenly a librarian at some point during his very long life is, again, one of those little details thrown into the story that almost seems to have no clear reason, or explanation, and yet, it keeps us mystified long after we're done reading. To make matters more confusing, Mr. Raven (Adam) can also take on different appearances; one moment he's a raven, and then he turns his back and becomes a man. His daughter, Mara, is also known as the cat-woman. Lilith often takes on the form of a spotted leopard, and a Persian cat, that is sometimes blue, white or gray. Satan is the great Shadow and also the black bat.

When Mr. Vane, during his second trip to the other world, first enters the "Bad Burrow", he comes upon a "metaphysical argument" in his mind (or someone else's) which takes the shape of an evil place of existence. Assumedly we get to look into a waking dream and see the turmoil that goes on

78

within. Here he also sees Lilith for the first time, and it may appear to some readers that he's seeing a glimpse of the future when he will meet her. (If C.S. Lewis were the author of the book you are now holding, he would likely add, "as in Mr. Dunne's sort of dreams").[3] However, there are many uncertainties that arise with that conception, the most obvious of which is, we don't know who's dream (mind) we're seeing into. Later in the book we find that when Mr. Vane enters the palace of the Queen (as Lilith is known to her townspeople) there is a black room that represents her brain, with red marks that symbolize veins, and he gets to see her thoughts and memories, including those pertaining to his time in the Bad Burrow. Curiously though, Mr. Vane is not present in these thoughts. This might lead us to conclude that the actions we saw in the Bad Burrow were things that took place in Lilith's mind instead of his own. Rather than think of it as a sort of daydream, we might do better to consider it an interior discussion (which admittedly is what most daydreams are), probably in the mind of Lilith, a struggle within her consciousness, a struggle being influenced by spiritual forces presenting themselves as urges. It's the same sort of struggle we all go through constantly, wrestling with our own demons (or "spots") and angels. Another reason we might assume that the struggle took place within the mind of Lilith is the extremely evil and violent nature of the Bad Burrow. It simply is not what we would expect to find in the mind of Mr. Vane.

Next Mr. Vane enters the "Evil Wood", and as the sun goes down, the trees and foliage around him begin to take on the appearance of living creatures in the darkness and the moonlight.

> Presently, to my listless roving gaze, the varied outlines of the clumpy foliage began to assume or imitate—say rather SUGGEST other shapes than their own. A light wind began to blow; it set the boughs of a

neighbour tree rocking, and all their branches aswing, every twig and every leaf blending its individual motion with the sway of its branch and the rock of its bough. Among its leafy shapes was a pack of wolves that struggled to break from a wizard's leash: greyhounds would not have strained so savagely! I watched them with an interest that grew as the wind gathered force, and their motions life.

Another mass of foliage, larger and more compact, presented my fancy with a group of horses' heads and forequarters projecting caparisoned from their stalls. Their necks kept moving up and down, with an impatience that augmented as the growing wind broke their vertical rhythm with a wilder swaying from side to side. What heads they were! how gaunt, how strange! — several of them bare skulls — one with the skin tight on its bones! One had lost the under jaw and hung low, looking unutterably weary — but now and then hove high as if to ease the bit. Above them, at the end of a branch, floated erect the form of a woman, waving her arms in imperious gesture. The definiteness of these and other leaf masses first surprised and then discomposed me: what if they should overpower my brain with seeming reality? But the twilight became darkness; the wind ceased; every shape was shut up in the night; I fell asleep.[4]

After this he awakens to the sound of a great battle raging around him between phantoms and skeletons, and as they fight they hurl insults at one another.

...skeleton jaws and phantom-throats swelled the deafening tumult with the war-cry of every opinion, bad or good, that had bred strife, injustice, cruelty in any world. The holiest words went with the most hating blow. Lie-distorted truths flew hurtling in the wind of javelins and bones. Every moment some one would turn against his comrades, and fight more wildly than before, THE TRUTH! THE TRUTH! still his cry. One I noted who wheeled ever in a circle, and smote on all sides.[5]

All the while Lilith is hovering above the battle, urging the men on in their fight with one another. This episode should not be taken as a cognizant event within the mind of Lilith or Mr. Vane either one. It is simply a glimpse of one pocket within the spirit world and how some of those who have not yet yielded to sleep in Adam's house of death still manage to go about healing their souls in thoughts and actions. We're told that Mr. Vane's grandfather is somewhere among these in the evil wood.

We'll see several examples of skeletons during Mr. Vanes journeys into the spirit world. Some have eyes—others not. Some have clothes; others are bare. Some have the power of speech while others are silent. And oddly enough, we'll find a humorous episode among two skeletons that are a divorced couple. It's odd in that some readers may find it to be somewhat out of place in this novel which is otherwise very dramatic. The male component of this couple is referred to (in a slanderous way) by the female once as "...my lord of Cokayne", surely referring to his having been an infidel during his material existence, a Don Juan sort of lord in a story created by Sir Aston Cokayne, who had carried on the Don Juan legend in his play— *The Tragedy of Ovid*, 1669. One of the funniest things MacDonald ever wrote is during this feud:

> "We are in the other world, I presume!"
> "Granted!—but in which or what sort of other world? This can't be hell!"
> "It must: there's marriage in it!...."[6]

C.S. LEWIS CALLED HIM MASTER

In this world on the other side of the looking glass, we find that there are many kinds of existences going on at once. Adam tells Mr. Vane that this couple, for instance, is in hell (remembering that MacDonald didn't believe in an *eternal* hell, nor one of Holy vengeance, but rather, one that was a sort of temporary refining fire): "You are not in hell ... Neither am I in hell. But those skeletons are in hell!"[7]

Adam then goes on to describe the character of the different conditions of skeletons in this world:

> "The male was never a gentleman," he went on, "and in the bony stage of retrogression, with his skeleton through his skin, and his character outside his manners, does not look like one. The female is less vulgar, and has a little heart. But, the restraints of society removed, you see them now just as they are and always were!"
>
> "Tell me, Mr. Raven, what will become of them," I said.
>
> "We shall see," he replied. "In their day they were the handsomest couple at court; and now, even in their dry bones, they seem to regard their former repute as an inalienable possession; to see their faces, however, may yet do something for them! They felt themselves rich too while they had pockets, but they have already begun to feel rather pinched! My lord used to regard my lady as a worthless encumbrance, for he was tired of her beauty and had spent her money; now he needs her to cobble his joints for him! These changes have roots of hope in them. Besides, they cannot now get far away from each other, and they see none else of their own kind: they must at last grow weary of their mutual repugnance, and begin to love one another!...."
>
> "I saw many more of their kind an hour ago, in the hall close by!" I said.

"Of their kind, but not of their sort," he answered. "For many years these will see none such as you saw last night. Those are centuries in advance of these. You saw that those could even dress themselves a little! It is true they cannot yet retain their clothes so long as they would—only, at present, for a part of the night; but they are pretty steadily growing more capable, and will by and by develop faces; for every grain of truthfulness adds a fibre to the show of their humanity. Nothing but truth can appear; and whatever is must seem."[8]

This last sentence helps us to understand much concerning the various looks of the skeletons, remembering that during the battle in the Evil Wood, while hurling insults at one another, one man said, "THE TRUTH! THE TRUTH!". The skeletons in this world, many working for hundreds of years or more, are going about the business of finding out who they are, and we're told later (in a quote from the bible) that everyone's true name is written on their foreheads but we cannot see it. And as they grow in mystical awareness of their own nature they will become visually more prominent with features, one day even gaining their faces, but not the mere masks they wore during earthly life, but rather, their true faces. In an earlier episode, before coming to the tragicomedy of the divorced couple, Mr. Vane witnesses a series of dances among skeletons during the night and says this afterward:

I rose and went among the apparitions, eager to understand something of their being and belongings. Were they souls, or were they and their rhythmic motions but phantasms of what had been? ... Did they know each how they appeared to the others—a death with living eyes? Had they used their faces, not for communication, not to utter thought and feeling, not to share existence with their neighbours, but to appear what they wished to appear, and conceal what they were? and, having made their faces masks, were they therefore deprived of those masks, and condemned to go without faces until they repented?

"How long must they flaunt their facelessness in faceless eyes?" I wondered. "How long will the frightful punition endure? Have they at length begun to love and be wise? Have they yet yielded to the shame that has found them?"[9]

Many people come to George MacDonald by way of C.S. Lewis, and the influence of MacDonald's storyline here concerning "faces" upon Lewis will be evident to many readers of Lewis's novel (perhaps his greatest), *Till We Have Faces*. Lewis shows, as does MacDonald, that dying to self in the Christian sense means, among other things—killing off our pretenses.

There is one other significant group of characters in our story, and that is the Little Lovers, and also to a lesser degree, the Bags. The Little Lovers appear to be children from the age of babies to teenagers. The Bags are the size of typical adult humans, but since the Little Lovers had never seen any other adults, the Bags seem like giants to them. When Mr. Vane first encounters the Little Lovers, he meets Lona among them, who seems to be a girl of about fifteen. She is much taller than the other children and probably the oldest. She is also quite beautiful, and Mr. Vane is quite taken with her. We learn later in the tale that her mother is Lilith, and that, Lilith was originally an angel that God gave to Adam for a wife. His second wife, Eve, however, was made in human form like her husband. According to many legends, including Jewish folklore, angels were frequently reported as being extremely tall—often about eight feet. Lilith in this story, is, like her daughter, very tall and very beautiful. But, her beauty is not from goodness, so her wickedness often gives her an ugly appearance. The Little Lovers represent for us Christians who have reached a place of complacency. Their physical growth has been stunted as a symbol of their spiritual stagnation. The Bags were formerly of the Little Lovers, but those who had given in to temptation and became wicked of their own free will. Lona explains this to Mr. Vane as best she can:

"The giants were not made always," she resumed. "If a Little One doesn't care, he grows greedy, and then lazy, and then big, and then stupid, and then bad. The dull creatures don't know that they come from us. Very few of them believe we are anywhere. They say *Nonsense!*—Look at little Blunty: he is eating one of their apples! He will be the next! Oh! oh! he will soon be big and bad and ugly, and not know it!"

The child stood by himself a little way off, eating an apple nearly as big as his head. I had often thought he did not look so good as the rest; now he looked disgusting.

"I will take the horrid thing from him!" I cried.

"It is no use," she answered... "it is too late! We were afraid he was growing, for he would not believe anything told him; but when he refused to share his berries, and said he had gathered them for himself, then we knew it! He is a glutton, and there is no hope of him...."

"Could not some of the boys watch him, and not let him touch the poisonous things?"

"He may have them if he will: it is all one—to eat the apples, and to be a boy that would eat them if he could. No; he must go to the giants! He belongs to them. You can see how much bigger he is than when first you came! He is bigger since yesterday."

...

"Does he want to be a giant?"

"He hates the giants, but he is making himself one all the same: he likes their apples! Oh baby, baby he was just such a darling as you when we found him!"

"He will be very miserable when he finds himself a giant!"

"Oh, no; he will like it well enough! That is the worst of it."

"Will he hate the Little Ones?"

"He will be like the rest; he will not remember us—most likely will not believe there are Little Ones. He will not care; he will eat his apples."[10]

However, the spiritual stagnation of the Little Lovers appears to be no fault of their own, but rather, because of the isolation in which they live from other people.

Pondering as I went, I recalled many traits of my little friends.

Once when I suggested that they should leave the country of the bad giants, and go with me to find another, they answered, "But that would be to not ourselves!"—so strong in them was the love of place that their country seemed essential to their very being! Without ambition or fear, discomfort or greed, they had no motive to desire any change; they knew of nothing amiss; and, except their babies, they had never had a chance of helping any one but myself:—How were they to grow?[11]

It becomes obvious throughout the story that the Little Lovers correspond to the reference Christ made in which he taught that we must all become like little children to come to the Father, to have belief and trust like children have in their parents. And thus, the above line about Blunty, "We were afraid he was growing, for he would not believe anything told him....", begins to make sense to us. The Little Lovers are trusting and charitable, and they are hopeful that Mr. Vane is the fulfillment of a prophecy. And while they seem courageous to a large degree, this is because they've had no reason to be afraid. When they first enter the city of the evil queen, Mr. Vane seems to think that this may be the first time the children have ever experienced fear. It could be that the children are full of the theological virtues of faith, hope and love, but are lacking in the natural virtues of wisdom, temperance, justice, and courage because they haven't had experiences in life which would produce these traits. St. Augustine said in *City of God* that the natural virtues could only develop after we have the theological virtues, so it may be that MacDonald is following this arrangement. Because of his life's experiences, Mr. Vane has much knowledge that he can teach the Little Lovers although he isn't sure what it is they need to learn, and he senses that in many ways the children are much ahead of him in spiritual growth, as is revealed later in Mr. Vane's conversation with Adam. Mr. Vane will, however, eventually (unwittingly) become the hand of God in guiding the children toward the development of the natural virtues.

"...but how could I teach them? I did not know how to begin. Besides, they were far ahead of me!"

"That is true. But you were not a rod to measure them with! Certainly, if they knew what you know, not to say what you might have known, they would be ahead of you—out of sight ahead! but you saw they were not growing—or growing so slowly that they had not yet developed the idea of growing! they were even afraid of growing!—You had never seen children remain children!"

"But surely I had no power to make them grow!"

"You might have removed some of the hindrances to their growing!"

"What are they? I do not know them. I did think perhaps it was the want of water!"

"Of course it is! they have none to cry with!"

"I would gladly have kept them from requiring any for that purpose!"

"No doubt you would—the aim of all stupid philanthropists! Why, Mr. Vane, but for the weeping in it, your world would never have become worth saving! You confess you thought it might be water they wanted: why did not you dig them a well or two?"

"That never entered my mind!"

"Not when the sounds of the waters under the earth entered your ears?"

"I believe it did once. But I was afraid of the giants for them. That was what made me bear so much from the brutes myself!"

"Indeed you almost taught the noble little creatures to be afraid of the stupid Bags! While they fed and comforted and worshipped you, all the time you submitted to be the slave of bestial men! You gave the darlings a seeming coward for their hero! A worse wrong you could hardly have done them. They gave you their hearts; you owed them your soul!—You might by this time have made the Bags hewers of wood and drawers of water to the Little Ones!"

"I fear what you say is true, Mr. Raven! But indeed I was afraid that more knowledge might prove an injury to them—render them less innocent, less lovely."

"They had given you no reason to harbour such a fear!"

"Is not a little knowledge a dangerous thing?"

"That is one of the pet falsehoods of your world! Is man's greatest knowledge more than a little?"[12]

GEORGE MACDONALD

Of course we learn toward the book's end that this water that's lacking throughout the land is the "River of Life" flowing out of heaven whereby all of humanity can get both the physical and spiritual nourishment it needs.

Admirers of C.S. Lewis will notice another important influence in Mr. Vane's relationship with Lona and the children. Those who have read Lewis's novel, *Perelandra*, will immediately see how much the naiveté that is present in Lona is similar to the same naiveté that is in the woman called Tinidril in the *Perelandra* adventure. Their manner of speech is very much the same. Something else the two novels have in common is the use of imagery, or lines of text from the Samuel Taylor Coleridge poem—*Kubla Khan*. Much of the imagery Lewis describes that Ransom sees during and shortly after emerging from the subterranean cavern in *Perelandra* seems right out the Coleridge poem. In the case of *Lilith*, MacDonald borrows quotes from the poem such as this when Adam reads from a book describing the life of Lilith, "For I had bathed in milk and honey-dew"[13]

From *Kubla Khan*:

> For he on honeydew hath fed,
> And drunk the milk of Paradise.[14]

Coleridge was a friend of MacDonald's father-in-law, as well as his uncle James. James MacDonald was in fact a surgeon who often made Coleridge angry by refusing to supply him with opium as a painkiller for his rheumatism. (Opium was just about the only drug known to relieve pain aside from alcohol in those days).

Lilith, with Mr. Vane's trip to another world, along with Lona's naiveté, plus her overall lack of knowledge and the way this presents itself through her manner of speech, was an inspiration on another writer that MacDonald would scarce like to be associated with—David Lindsay. (Lindsay once admitted the influence of MacDonald in an interview). His sci-fi novel, *A Voyage To Arcturus*, is full sway of the literary vehicles MacDonald had used in *Lilith*. And, like C.S. Lewis, Lindsay places his main characters on another planet and has a female portraiture that corresponds to Lona. Her name is Joiwind, she's very tall, very naïve, and she speaks in the same short, stabby, childlike sentences as Lona. The odd thing is, that, Lindsay's novel is nothing short of a Gnostic Treatise. C.S. Lewis, in a letter, once referred to *Arcturus* as being nearly diabolical and so Manichean as to be almost Satanic. However, for some strange reason, Lewis originally got the idea of writing the first entry of his space trilogy after reading Lindsay's book even though he detested Lindsay's philosophy. Why he didn't get the idea from reading *Lilith* just as Lindsay had (considering Lewis had already read *Lilith* first) is an imponderable.

The only city from the world beyond the glass that we learn about in detail is Bulika, which would seem to represent Babylon. Mr. Vane says:

> A few minutes more, and I could discern, against the pale aurora, the wall-towers of a city—seemingly old as time itself.
>
> ...
>
> Around the city were gardens....[15]

So it would appear that we have a reference here to Babylon, one of the oldest cities the world has known and its famous hanging gardens.[16] We might also consider the role that this city and its evil queen, Lilith, play in their connection with the bible. Much of the book's end is taken from Revelation. In the biblical apocalypse, Babylon may represent Rome, but it has an overarching meaning, not only in Revelation but also in other books, as being symbolic of any people group that is corrupt and overindulgent. We also find in Revelation the dreamlike imagery of a woman/prostitute *who sits on many waters*. According to the angel who interprets this passage in the bible, the waters signify multitudes of peoples and nations. Lilith has much of the water that formerly flowed from the great River of Life in heaven held tight in an egg in her hand, and because of this the people in the world beyond the glass are spiritually dead or dying. But, we must remember that this other world is the spirit world that we all live in and are a part of, unseen though it is. The forgetfulness, naiveté, ignorance, and lack of wisdom found throughout this other world also affects us in our material world of three dimensions.

The prostitute of the bible who represents Babylon, which in turn symbolizes the overindulgence of a corrupt group of people, is portrayed as being adorned with gold, pearls, and other precious stones. Lilith in our story starts her corruption of the townsfolk by teaching them to dig for precious stones and to sell them to neighboring peoples. She also teaches them to love riches and to hate both poverty and those who are impoverished. In time, the people grow so corrupt and lazy that they actually consider it a "disgrace to work".

We're told that the River of Life in *Lilith*, of which there is a stream from it found flowing out of a rock in a cave, is very warm and metallic tasting. It could be that the metallic taste is a reference to Babylon again, as Babylon was a city known for its advanced techniques in metallurgy. It's a possibility that the water is warm because it flows from the throne of God. (Ezekiel and Revelation both mention the water flowing from under the throne of God). According to Revelation, God and the Lamb (Christ) will be the "light" of the new heavens and new earth, and there will be no need for a sun any longer. Whether this light from God produces heat, and whether the river flowing from the throne is heated by its proximity to the throne, are both easily debatable, but it may offer an explanation for the water's heat.

During the trip to Heaven by Mr. Vane and the children at the book's end, Mr. Vane says that, "Sense after sense hitherto asleep, awoke in me—sense after sense indescribable...."[17]

It's mentioned very early on in the novel that beings on the other side of the glass live in the land of seven dimensions and ten senses. They can travel very quickly there compared to travel in our three dimensional world because they can "pull up the plumb-line" of gravity. Many readers and scholars have poured over the text looking for a more specific meaning in these words. What does MacDonald mean by seven dimensions, ten senses, and pulling up the plumb-line of gravity and letting the world "spin round under your feet"? The last one seems easy enough. If we could stay in one place without feeling the gravitational effects of the Earth, the land would buzz past us at more than 17,000-miles-per-hour while the Earth rotated on its axis. Further, if we stand apart from the Earth's orbit around the sun, it would fly out of sight at nearly 70,000-mile-per-hour while other planets orbit closer and closer to us until they overtake us, and eventually the Earth would come back to where it began. Taking this analogy further we could say that every galaxy is also rotating (which they are, albeit it very slowly in comparison to what the solar system *seems*), and that, if we could stay in one place within the known universe, much of it that is a great distance away would come to us very quickly without us ever having to move an inch. Add to this the way time and space may interact in a region of many dimensions and the possibilities are extraordinary.

Trying to address the problem of the seven dimensions and ten senses is a bit trickier. Many scholars have tried to offer plausible explanations but none seem to have come up with a satisfying answer for many of us. How ever many dimensions there are, both in the story and in real life, the fact remains that this story takes place in at least one that is very different than the three (or four if you're one of those who count time as a dimension) we're used to. Mr. Vane first learns that this other world is in another dimension when Adam (as the raven) informs him that a tree he sees in this other world is also standing on the hearth of his kitchen simultaneously. But, to simply refer to this other world as being in another dimension would be unconsidered. This other world has at least the same three *kinds* of dimensions (length, width, depth) that our world does, so the world beyond the glass is actually a multidimensional world rather than simply another dimension of ours. If we count three dimensions in each world plus time as another that is connected to both, we have a total of seven dimensions. And, if we count that beings have five bodily senses in each world, that would make a total of ten senses. This could possibly be what MacDonald means.

Another thing to consider is that the novel follows many events and terminologies present in the book of Revelation. In the apocalypse, the numbers ten and seven come up time and again. MacDonald may have simply been pointing us to the book of Revelation by choosing these numbers for his dimensions and senses rather than having anything specifically in mind as to what these extra dimensions and senses are. And, in fact, as quoted above, when Mr. Vane and the children reach Heaven and enter into the experience of having "sense after sense" awoken within them, along with the detail in which MacDonald goes into trying to describe the indescribable, it would seem likely that he is merely passing on to us, in a poetic and undetermined way, the notion of what *many* senses and dimensions would be like. It's quite possible that these numbers are meaningless in themselves and are there merely to convey a sensation of *many* things, feelings, and experiences that "no eye has seen, nor ear has heard". He may be only enticing us with wonder and in the process helping to "baptize our imaginations", as Lewis once said of reading MacDonald. Mostly, he wants to bring out a sense of *otherness* that lay deep within us all. Other than pointing us to the book of Revelation, the actual numbers may very likely be irrelevant.

C.S. LEWIS CALLED HIM MASTER

Adam seems to have an ability to see and hear in both worlds at once. Lilith also seems to, if not see and hear, at least be able to perceive things in both worlds, as is demonstrated when she sends Mr. Vane up a tree near her palace, and by which, Mr. Vane will come out into a fountain at his own home in our world—she will follow after him. It seems to be premeditated on her part. No one else demonstrates this ability of dual perception except Adam and Lilith. When Mr. Vane cannot hear a child playing the piano at his home while standing in the other world, Adam says, "Pardon me: I forgot your deafness." This may be taken as a suggestion that Mr. Vane should also, and perhaps will one day, be able to perceive things in both worlds simultaneously. It may allude to spiritual growth and what Christians refer to as "gifts of the Spirit", which endow mankind (when they are a new kind of man) with abilities to perceive things in this world and in the spirit world around us, and to have new kinds of abilities to effect change in this, or perhaps *both*, worlds. Jesus was the first of a new kind of man who had these abilities that all new men can have when they are remade. One of those abilities he demonstrated was clairvoyance, also called second sight, or more recently—remote viewing. In John 1:48, Jesus told Nathaniel that he saw him under a fig tree before ever having met him or seen him with his physical eyes. This in fact was the reason Nathaniel chose to believe in and become a follower of Jesus. But clairvoyance is just the tip of the Spiritual iceberg; healing, visions, auditions, dreams/interpretations, perhaps even moving mountains and walking on water are within reach of the new man.

Some people refer to the spirit world as being something that lies within man, or within the mind of man. Others tell us that all worlds and beings are ultimately within God's mind and are sustained by his thoughts. Let us recall again that passage from St. Paul, "In him we live and move and have our being." *Lilith* definitely leaves us with the notion that everything in the end is pure thought, "'Perhaps it may comfort you,' said the raven, 'to be told that you have not yet left your house, neither has your house left you. At the same time it cannot contain you, or you inhabit it!'"[18]

Or as Mr. Vane says to himself after his first trip to the spirit world:

> ...what is there to secure me against my own brain? Can I tell what it is even now generating?—what thought it may present me the next moment, the next month, or a year away? What is at the heart of my brain? What is behind my think? Am I there at all?—Who, what am I?[19]

He asks himself these questions after realizing in the other world that he can no longer remember his own name, and that, without a name, or such things as jobs and hobbies and relatives to identify ourselves with, we are left with nothing that tells us who we are. Adam (as the raven) explains:

> "No one can say he is himself, until first he knows that he is, and then what himself is. In fact, nobody is himself, and himself is nobody. There is more in it than you can see now, but not more than you need to see. You have, I fear, got into this region too soon, but none the less you must get to be at home in it; for home, as you may or may not know, is the only place where you can go out and in. There are places you can go into, and places you can go out of; but the one place, if you do but find it, where you may go out and in both, is home."[20]

And home seems to be a place of pure thought. When toward the end of the book Mr. Vane finally lies down to sleep in Adam's death chamber, he says:

C.S. LEWIS CALLED HIM MASTER

For centuries I dreamed—or was it chiliads? or only one long night?—But why ask? for time had nothing to do with me; I was in the land of thought—farther in, higher up [readers may see a connection here with C.S. Lewis's last *Narnia* tale and Aslan's cry of, "Further up, further in", while the children traveled through heavenly worlds after they died.] than the seven dimensions, the ten senses: I think I was where I am—in the heart of God.[21]

The thought behind what MacDonald teaches here is nothing new to the Christian Mystical tradition. That everything is in the mind of God is something that most mystics, even outside of Christianity, conclude from their experiences it seems. Blake's notion that there may be a multitude of universes in the palm of a man's hand may have had a strong effect on the thinking of MacDonald and his writing of *Lilith*. Add to this what Greville says in his biography:

But my father did unquestionably get help from Blake in his need to tell us the truth about the grave. ...

For as long as I can remember there hung in my father's study four of Blake's illustrations to Blair's Grave—the good man dead on his tomblike bed, the bad man fiercely escaping with evil spirits, the Spirit of man with the candle of the Lord searching all the Grave's inward parts, and the old man driven—the North Wind blowing where it listeth—into his tomb, to find himself reborn into the fullness of youth, with head uplifted to the risen sun....

I cannot doubt that my father, though he knew little of Blake beyond his lyrics, lit upon through him the idea of the cemetery in Lilith.[22]

GEORGE MACDONALD

The notion of the world and everything in it being composed of thought, and that thought being in the mind of God, is not without its weaknesses. One question plaguing our conscience might be that of evil existing in God's mind. Can we any longer call God good if evil lives within him? This may have been a question that MacDonald mulled over as well. MacDonald often used beauty to signify God's presence within an individual. He does this in *Lilith* with both Eve and Mara. But, he also asks in several of his books, including *Lilith* and *Phantastes*, how certain things (usually represented by women in his novels) can be so outwardly beautiful, and yet so full of evil as in the case of Lilith. It turns his world topsy-turvy.

Another problem is that of free will. The Hindus, and many Greeks also, believed that everything existed within an eternal absolute being of pure thought. But it's difficult to come to terms with how a world of created beings existing within this one supreme being's thoughts could still have any form of free will. If our thoughts are ultimately within God's thoughts then can we really call them our own? Would not the Calvinists be closer to the truth of the matter in this case and predestination be a certainty? Some may conjecture that, however we choose to view the matter, it will probably come to nil in the end. They might say that, whether we live in the mind of God or as an outside entity, we would never be any the wiser for it anyway. However, we cannot say that it would have no effect on how we live our lives, whether or not we are wise to the fact. It would have a great consequence on the choices we make and how we conduct ourselves. The question is: Do we truly have free will or do we act out a written script? And would we know the difference? But ours is a world of hope, faith, and trust—not of knowing. That is left to God, and we must do the best we can.

Mr. Vane has one acquaintance that accompanies him throughout most of his journey and that is the moon. In actuality he finds there is more than one moon in the spirit world. But, whichever moon is with him, that moon will act in accordance with his current attitude(s) and mindset. It acts almost like a mother watching her children at play. If he needs protection, she protects. If he needs a friendly face, she turns it to him. If he needs scolding, she may turn her face from him completely and leave him to his own devices. This happens once when he gets caught up in his own selfish desire to ride a wonderful horse owned by Adam. But, he rides off at a time and place that Adam forbids, saying to himself all the while, that he's riding off to try and protect the Little Lovers from Lilith who has just left in search of them, but in his deepest heart he knows that, really he's become intoxicated with the power of the magnificent beast beneath him. So he disobeys Adam, refuses to sleep a night in his chamber of death, and rides off toward the land of the children. As he goes, however, he watches his companion, the moon, take a nose dive over the horizon and out of sight. Now he is left vulnerable to the evil creatures of the night that would have never bothered him while the moon was there to protect him. "Light and darkness can have no place together." All comes right at the end however, and he is one step closer to learning obedience and trust.

Lilith is possibly the most complicated character within the novel although she doesn't realize it herself. Unlike Eve, she was once an angel, but she grew evil and even killed herself to get away from Adam's presence.

> One child, indeed, she bore; then, puffed with the fancy that she had created her, would have me fall down and worship her! Finding, however, that I would but love and honour, never obey and worship her, she poured out her blood to escape me, fled to the army of the aliens, and soon had so ensnared the heart of the great Shadow, that he became her slave, wrought her will, and made her queen of Hell.[23]

So, she took up residence with demons (aliens/shadows) as a bodiless spirit and became entangled with Satan, and Satan became so infatuated with her that, "...he became her slave". This is a little confusing though because MacDonald makes it plain throughout the rest of the story that it's Lilith who is enslaved to Satan (the Great Shadow) and not the other way round. It's difficult to determine why MacDonald stated things differently in this section of the novel unless he simply got confused himself. This is not too hard to believe when we consider both his age and how many times he rewrote this book before coming to the final draft.

Lilith is only able to live in a body of flesh if she has, every now and then, the blood of a human to feed upon. This of course puts her in the arena of vampirism. While MacDonald was not an author of the horror genre, he did on rare occasion write a tale about vampires, werewolves, demonic shadows, and the like, so this was nothing new for him. Lilith primarily fed on the blood of children. This accomplished a twofold rationale. It brought her the blood she needed to physically manifest herself, and it also gave her the opportunity to try to kill her own child, Lona, whom she had not seen in many years and could probably not identify. Killing as many children as she could, she might kill Lona in the process. Lilith believed (although we aren't told why she believes this) that the birth of children was connected to the death of the parents, at least in her spiritual world, that her own immortality would be at stake as long as her daughter, Mara, lived. At times Lilith took the form of a spotted leopard to kill. Other times, Satan, as the Great Shadow, would go out into the night and procure a child for her. The white leopard would often follow him however, and try to get to the child and lead it to safety before he could carry out his mission.

Speaking of the white leopard and the spotted white leopard (both female leopardesses), we know that the identity of the spotted one is Lilith herself. The other is harder to come to any conclusions about. When we first meet this white leopard, she has bounded from a window in the house of Mara (the cat woman). Mara calls this white leopard by the name Asarte. We know that there are creatures at Mara's house that are made from the imaginations of people who sleep there, and apparently Asarte is one of them. Unfortunately, because the name Asarte is so well known, and there are so many derivatives that come from it (Artemis, Ashtart, Athenais, Ashtoret etc.), and because of the many divergent stories surrounding her, it's very difficult to have any full understanding of why MacDonald used this name in the text or how she directly relates to other characters in the story. For those who have read the original first draft of *Lilith*, (a story very different from the final draft) we know that Asarte was yet another side of Lilith, so that the two leopards represented different aspects of her. If that was still MacDonald's idea in this final draft, we have precious few hints of it.

There are some aspects of the legend of Asarte that may help us, but only a little. Asarte is normally associated with the Phoenician god Baal. They are the male and female counterpart to one another in some religious cultures. Sometimes they're represented as evil, other times good. Asarte in Greek mythology under the name Artemis, was said to be the friend and protector of youth. This would certainly correspond with the way the white leopard protected the babies from Satan and Lilith. Artemis's counterpart, Baal, was among both Hebrew and other Semitic peoples, generally thought of as a fertility god, and one who was especially associated with rain and water. The Talmud in some parts, refers to Baal as a god of subterraneous waters. But while the subterraneous waters of Baal, and the underground waters in the novel, may seem on the surface to have some correlation, it's hard to determine just how the two would be connected. It's also hard to figure out how Lilith and Asarte could have been associated together in

GEORGE MACDONALD

MacDonald's mind to the point of him making them parts of the same person's characteristic makeup in the first draft of *Lilith*.

The spots on Lilith, both as the leopard and the one she carries with her as a woman, probably represent both sin and demonic forces at work within her. They're a blemish to her otherwise beautiful form. "Wickedness has made her ugly!", says Mr. Vane to the children when they question her beauty. The bible tells us that Christ comes back for a "spotless bride" (church).

According to MacDonald's theology, all people must sleep in Adam's house of death and be reborn, even Satan himself. None would perish in the end. This is not without some biblical backing. "For as in Adam all die, so also in Christ shall all be made alive." Of course there are other biblical writings which read contrary to this one.

G.K. Chesterton, probably under the influence of MacDonald, tells a similar tale of all mankind being redeemed in the end. It's in his novel—*The Ball and the Cross*. The final page tells of two men dropping from an airship piloted by Professor Lucifer (obviously the Devil). They crash into a fire that's raging in a building below.

> "They are gone!" screamed Beatrice, hiding her head. "O God! they are lost!"
>
> Evan put his arm about her, and remembered his own vision.
>
> "No, they are not lost," he said. "They are saved. He has taken away no souls with him, after all."
>
> He looked vaguely about the fire that was already fading, and there among the ashes lay two shining things that had survived the fire, his sword and Turnbull's, fallen haphazard in the pattern of a cross.[24]

Chesterton leaves us with the impression that the two men, both of whom had been on the side of Lucifer, had for some reason in the end preferred to die than go off in the airship with him. And, that final decision is their redemption. But Chesterton does not go so far as to suggest that Satan himself will be saved from a hellish separation from God for all eternity. And indeed it is only a hope in MacDonald. But, it seemed logical in his mind, especially after having read Jacob Bohme and listening to his pastor-friend F.D. Maurice, both of whom believed that all of creation lived in the mind of God, and thus, even in deepest hell one must live within God. We must try to remember though, that while MacDonald read some of the writings of Swedenborg, Bohme, Blake, Novalis and probably even some of those writings which we might call Gnostic today, still he in no way suggested that everything these rebel thinkers taught was to be taken as truth. (He actually read precious little of Swedenborg and Blake). While some of their learning would avail itself to the much more radical and dangerous occultist theories as espoused by Theosophists groups, MacDonald seems to have had very little use for these societies or their more discordant teachings. Even though he had himself written a story about clairvoyance, *The Portent*, he was disturbed when he once found himself in the company of a clairvoyant, one who had shown at least some proof of her powers to his friend, John Ruskin.[25] MacDonald's clairvoyant in *The Portent* was a very saintly old lady of the Christian faith who was simply gifted by the Spirit with something not at all unlike what Christ did when he saw Nathaniel under the tree as we discussed earlier. There is nothing in MacDonald's books that shows the same improper envy for spiritual *secrets* and power that Spiritualism is noted for. He had the special and rare ability to simply take good from whatever source he came across and reject the bad, being careful never to throw out the baby with the bathwater. Even the vilest of men might say or write something noble on occasion, and, if they did, MacDonald wouldn't hesitate to pick up on it and use it.

GEORGE MACDONALD

When Lilith is taken to Mara's house of dreams, there are many references throughout the night to the essential elements—air, water, and fire, but not earth, at least not directly, but earth is probably taken for granted as that which gives us a body and material existence. The air and water come soundless and without physical force, yet they seem to take hold of Lilith and float her on the settle (bench). She immediately begins to think with thoughts that are in strife, herself against herself (or so it seems to her). Her intellect and her emotions, as symbolized by air and water, are stripped down to something so raw and ancient that she soon realizes they are not her own—that she indeed has no real thoughts of her own and never has (imagination belongs to God). Hers is but the will to choose between various ideas placed in her mind by God's assistants. Once she is penetrated by the white-hot worm (the essential fire that is the heart of the world) she can see herself through the eye's of God for what she truly is. She begins to see that what she thought was her own will was not— that there was a part of her that was still good, and *that* part of her, long ago forgotten, still has a voice behind the pseudo-will which is that of the Great Shadow, something she had listened to for so long that she thought it was her own. She must, for God will make her, learn to strengthen that voice—that will behind the will. But she can only do so much, put it in God's hands, and allow him to do the rest. This is true redemption. It's a surrendering of the will.

Clergymen have long argued that this is essentially what makes a Christian a Christian. It is not about believing in a magic name. Nor about belief in Christ alone. As many have pointed out, even the Devil believes; actually—he knows. Even when we come to the point where we really do wish to be good, to do good, to hate evil, we find that we can only do so much. Lilith cannot open her hand, cannot let go of her last sin. It's too much for her. Many times we hear someone say, "I want to, but—I don't want to", or, "I know I should, but—I just can't". We

103

know we should want to help out our poor old neighbor lady with chores around her home, and we wish that we did want to. Yet, we'd also like to be doing something else altogether. But the very fact that we wish we could change our selfish desires into selfless ones shows that we have a will behind our will, a desire behind our desire. That's what MacDonald is telling us here. And, like Lilith, there are some things we just cannot let go of on our own. But when the essential fire of the universe that is God gets inside us deeper and deeper, it becomes a refining fire and remakes us. For this final act to take place, Lilith must now leave Mara's home and go to sleep in Adam's house of death, where she, like us, will die unto life.

Another admirer of MacDonald whose works may have been influenced by *Lilith* was Charles Williams (full name: Charles Walter Stansby Williams), an author and editor at Oxford University Press, and the best friend of C.S. Lewis for many years. Williams included a poem by MacDonald entitled "The Yerl o' Waterydeck" in *A Book of Victorian Narrative Verse*, a volume he edited for Oxford Press and published in 1927, almost a decade before he would meet C.S. Lewis. Whether or not Williams had any familiarity at this time with any of MacDonald's work other than his poetry is unknown. However, Lewis, one of MacDonald's biggest fans, would surely have filled Williams in on what he knew and admired in MacDonald's books after the two men met in 1936. Williams only wrote two of his seven novels after 1936, *Descent into Hell*— 1937, and *All Hallows' Eve*—1945. Both novels have many elements within them that give the impression that Williams had studied *Lilith* at least to some degree. Mr. Vane says during his second trip to the spirit world, "But how was life to be lived in a world of which I had all the laws to learn?"[26] Those familiar with the Williams stories will recall how very often he echoed this same refrain in one way or another right from his very first novel. The most striking similarities come during Lilith's stay at Mara's cottage when she first begins her transformation from evil to good. The entire chapter reads very much like something out of a Williams story, with the cloudy presences that are felt more than seen, or the feeling of wind and water filling the house but neither seen nor heard. These things are instead sensed with the minds of the people who are present rather than with their physical bodies. At one point there's a feeling of absolute nothingness that enters the room, and Mr. Vane gives us his recollection of it:

> Gradually my soul grew aware of an invisible darkness, a something more terrible than aught that had yet made itself felt. A horrible Nothingness, a Negation positive infolded her; the border of its being that was yet no being, touched me, and for one ghastly instant I seemed alone with Death Absolute! It was not the absence of everything I felt, but the presence of Nothing. The princess dashed herself from the settle to the floor with an exceeding great and bitter cry. It was the recoil of Being from Annihilation.[27]

At this point the nothingness is something which is *around* Lilith. Soon she will experience something a little different; she feels the creative fire of the universe, God himself, move out of her, and she is left in utter darkness. Yet, she is not dead. Indeed, nothing can ever truly die. She is simply in the void, free of all contemplation and action. Her mind has no thoughts and yet—it exists.

> Then came the most fearful thing of all. I did not know what it was; I knew myself unable to imagine it; I knew only that if it came near me I should die of terror! I now know that it was Life in Death—life dead, yet existent; and I knew that Lilith had had glimpses, but only glimpses of it before: it had never been with her until now.

...Mara went and sat down by the fire. Fearing to stand alone with the princess, I went also and sat again by the hearth. Something began to depart from me. A sense of cold, yet not what we call cold, crept, not into, but out of my being, and pervaded it. The lamp of life and the eternal fire seemed dying together, and I about to be left with naught but the consciousness that I had been alive. Mercifully, bereavement did not go so far, and my thought went back to Lilith.

Something was taking place in her which we did not know. We knew we did not feel what she felt, but we knew we felt something of the misery it caused her. The thing itself was in her, not in us; its reflex, her misery, reached us, and was again reflected in us: she was in the outer darkness, we present with her who was in it! We were not in the outer darkness; had we been, we could not have been with her; we should have been timelessly, spacelessly, absolutely apart. The darkness knows neither the light nor itself; only the light knows itself and the darkness also. None but God hates evil and understands it.

Something was gone from her, which then first, by its absence, she knew to have been with her every moment of her wicked years. The source of life had withdrawn itself; all that was left her of conscious being was the dregs of her dead and corrupted life.

She stood rigid. Mara buried her head in her hands. I gazed on the face of one who knew existence but not love—knew nor life, nor joy, nor good; with my eyes I saw the face of a live death! She knew life only to know that it was dead, and that, in her, death lived. It was not merely that life had ceased in her, but that she was consciously a dead thing. She had killed her life, and was dead—and knew it. She must death it for ever and ever! She had tried her hardest to unmake herself, and could not! she was a dead life! she could not cease! she must be! In her face I saw and read beyond its misery—saw in its dismay that the dismay behind it was more than it could manifest. It sent out a livid gloom; the light that was in her was darkness, and after its kind it shone. She was what God could not have created. She had usurped beyond her share in self-creation, and her part had undone His! She saw now what she had made, and behold, it was not good! She was as a conscious corpse, whose coffin would never come to pieces, never set her free! Her bodily eyes stood wide open, as if gazing into the heart of horror essential—her own indestructible evil. Her right hand also was now clenched—upon existent Nothing—her inheritance![28]

Anyone who has read Charles Williams brilliant novel, *Descent Into Hell* would quickly see the similarity here. Witness the final chapter from *Descent Into Hell*:

He shrank into himself, trying to shut his eyes and lose sight of this fearful opposite of the world he had known. Quite easily he succeeded. But he could not close his ears, for he did not know how to manage the more complex co-ordination of shoulders and arms and hands. So there entered into him still a small, steady, meaningless flow of sound, which stung and tormented him with the same lost knowledge of meaning; small burning flames flickered down on his soul. His eyes opened again in mere despair. A little hopeless voice came from his throat. He said, and rather gasped than spoke: 'Ah! ah!' Then everything at which he was looking rushed together and became a point, very far off, and he also was a point opposite it; and both points were rushing together, because in this place they drew towards each other from the more awful repulsion of the void. But fast as they went they never reached one another, for out of the point that was not he there expanded an anarchy of unintelligible shapes and hid it, and he knew it had gone out, expiring in the emptiness before it reached him. The shapes turned themselves into alternate panels of black and white. He had forgotten the name of them, but somewhere at some time he had thought he knew similar forms and they had had names. These had no names, and whether they were or were not anything, and whether that anything was desirable or hateful he did not know. He had now no consciousness of himself as such, for the magical mirrors of Gomorrah had been broken, and the city itself had been blasted, and he was out beyond it in the blankness of a living oblivion, tormented by oblivion. The shapes stretched out beyond him, all half turned away, all rigid and silent. He was sitting at the end, looking up an avenue of nothingness, and the little flames licked his soul, but they did not now come from without, for they were the power, and the only power, his dead past had on him; the life, and the only life, of his soul. There was, at the end of the grand avenue, a bobbing shape of black and white that hovered there and closed it. As he saw it there came on him a suspense; he waited for something to happen. The silence lasted; nothing happened. In that pause expectancy faded. Presently then the shape went out and he was drawn, steadily, everlastingly, inward and down through the bottomless circles of the void.[29]

In Williams' *All Hallows' Eve*, the villain of the novel is a man called Simon, often referred to as—the Clerk, (he was a clergyman but not a Christian). His character is largely based on the legend of St. Germain, a man known throughout Europe a few hundred years ago who was said to have worked great miracles, and to have either never died, or to at least have lived for several hundred years. Simon, at the book's end, has made for himself an enchanted circle from which to perform his diabolism. But, "The City", the Holy network of relationships and correspondences that runs between the spirit world and the material world, has other plans for him. He had earlier created two doppelgangers to do his bidding (through bi-location) at other parts of the world. But, a hard and terrible rain sent from heaven comes right through the roof, and he begins to descend into the dimensions of hell along with his doppelgangers who had gathered around him. The rain from heaven is his demise, but it is life to those who have given themselves to The City and surrendered their wills to God, and those flourish in it, even work miracles in it. In *Lilith*, the water from heaven is of course a river running from under the throne of God. It also gives life. And there is also the connection of the water from heaven to baptism in both stories. One will find many such associations between *Lilith* and the final two Williams novels.

Lilith, at one point, desires to cease living but finds that she cannot. Indeed that nothing can cease *being* but can only change. Oddly, the Character, Lionel, in an earlier Williams novel—*War in Heaven*—asks of Prester John that he may be granted annihilation one day. Williams' friend and biographer, Alice Mary Hadfield, has stated that this character, Lionel, is the one who was most like Charles Williams himself in real life. Indeed, Williams stated in at least two essays (which can be found in "Image of the City", a collection of his essays) that he felt no special regard for life itself. He confided to his friend C.S. Lewis that if it had not been for the Incarnation, whereby God himself thought it bearable to come and partake in his own creation (a creation which the Bible's tells us he referred to as "good" in Genesis), that it never would have dawned on him that existence in itself was a good thing, and that, given the choice he would rather not have it. However, he did hold out a hope that there was something in him, in all of us, outside of this material existence, that *chose* to be here—that there may be much more to the situation than we can now know.

Concerning the River of Life being present in *Lilith*, it might not be too presumptuous of us to wonder whether or not Robert Lowry's now famous hymn, "Shall We Gather At the River", had any influence thereof. It was first published in 1865 and would have been a song that MacDonald himself might very likely have sung and known a great deal about. It was well-known in Scotland, and MacDonald would surely have heard the hymn sung during his American lecture tour which commenced only a few short years after the song was first published in America. Henry S. Burrage wrote of how Lowry came to write the song in his book from 1888, *Baptist Hymn Writers and Their Hymns*.

The hymn

"Shall we gather at the river"

was written one afternoon in July, 1864, when Dr. Lowry was pastor of the Hanson Place Baptist church, Brooklyn, N.Y. The weather was oppressively hot, and the author was lying on a lounge in a state of physical exhaustion. He was almost incapable of bodily exertion, and his imagination began to take to itself wings. Visions of the future passed before him with startling vividness. The imagery of the Apocalypse took the form of tableaux. Brightest of all were the throne, the heavenly river, and the gathering of the saints. While he was thus breathing heavily in the sultry atmosphere of that July day, his soul seemed to take new life from that celestial outlook. He began to wonder why the hymn-writers had said so much about "the river of death," and so little about "the pure river of water of life, clear as crystal, proceeding out of the throne of God and of the

GEORGE MACDONALD

Lamb." As he mused, the words began to construct themselves.

At the end of her stay in Mara's House of Dreams, Lilith is very near to her transformation. As she lay and wept, a gentle wind blew about and enveloped her as though she were in the everlasting Sea that is God, and indeed she was. She began to be conscious of that great Sea in everything around her, even the sounds of everyday things took on new meaning for her as MacDonald beautifully puts it.

> She ... began to listen. For in the skirts of the wind had come the rain—the soft rain that heals the mown, the many-wounded grass—soothing it with the sweetness of all music, the hush that lives between music and silence. It bedewed the desert places around the cottage, and the sands of Lilith's heart heard it, and drank it in... soon she was fast asleep.[30]

The "hush that lives between music and silence" is another old expression from the early Christian Mystical writers who claimed that God is in that hush more than in the sounds, assumedly because the sounds come from a place of silence to begin with, and that silence seems to be the foundation which sounds rest upon. Christian Mystics regard the biblical passages about rest and silence with particular fancy. "Be still and know that I am God", for instance, or the way God came to Elijah by, "a still small voice", rather than the whirlwind, earthquake, and fire that preceded it. For the mystics, rest and stillness are the pillars of existence. What scientists regard as nothingness, mystics regard as the Absolute. We might extend this line of reasoning much further. Many of the things that makeup the human experience, the most important things, are items that have no material existence and are frequently unexplainable, such as emotions. Some might say that true joy from God was simply a gift that came without warning and for no reason, often when you least expected it. It was being happy without cause. Joy was a key component of C.S. Lewis's conversion process. He saw that joy was not in having a thing longed for but was actually in the waiting and the longing itself. T.S. Eliot said something similar along these lines in *Four Quartets*:

> I said to my soul, be still; wait without hope
> For hope would be hope for the wrong thing;
> wait without love
> For love would be love of the wrong thing; there
> is yet faith
> But the faith and the love and the hope are all in
> the waiting.

Mara, Mr. Vane, the children, and Lilith all depart for Adam's house where all must go one day, to its endless room of couches where we will dream the good dreams that lead to repentance, and where the Great Shadow which is Satan cannot disturb our slumber. Lilith must open her hand and relinquish the waters of heaven she has held for a thousand years before she can sleep. Mara tells her that until she opens her hand, "You may think you are dead, but it will only be a dream; you may think you have come awake, but it will still be only a dream. Open your hand, and you will sleep indeed—then wake indeed."[31] This borrows from Blake and his notion that we are all asleep in the same dream. C.S. Lewis borrowed ideas from both writers about our current state of affairs being more of a dream than a waking existence. He thought that heaven would be a condition of blessed wakefulness, so much so, that we would look back on our present earthly existence as being little more than a dream. Of course Novalis said similar things much earlier yet.

But Lilith simply cannot seem to open her hand. Eventually she remembers that Adam has a sword that the angel who had once guarded the gate to Eden gave to him, and she asks him to get the sword and cut off her hand. Adam complies with her request, and no sooner did he strike the blow than she was fast asleep. In his description of the sword, MacDonald writes, "The scabbard looked like vellum grown dark with years, but the hilt shone like gold that nothing could tarnish."[32] The light which flashed from the sword made Lilith open her eyes just before her hand was severed. Afterwards, Mr. Vane asks Adam, "Will you not dress the wound?" Adam replies that, "A wound from this sword needs no dressing. It is healing and not hurt."[33]

We might conjecture from this that the sword is a symbol of the word of truth as St. Paul says:

> For the word of God is living and active. Sharper than any double-edged sword, it penetrates even to dividing soul and spirit, joints and marrow; it judges the thoughts and attitudes of the heart. Nothing in all creation is hidden from God's sight. Everything is uncovered and laid bare before the eyes of him to whom we must give account. Hebrews 4:12-13

This last sentence describes exactly what happens to Lilith now that her hand is loosed by the sword, and she is asleep in the land of God's Holy Dreams. The sword's scabbard looking like, "vellum grown dark with years", surely represents the bible, as old books often used vellum for a book's binding. The sword and its handle gleaming, "that nothing could tarnish", would then symbolize the truth of the words in the ancient book, words and truth that would never die.

Lilith asks Eve about the sword: "There was a sword I once saw in your husband's hands ... I fled when I saw it. I heard him who bore it say it would divide whatever was not one and indivisible."[34] This doubtless is a reference to the above scripture, "it penetrates even to dividing soul and spirit, joints and marrow".

A little later, Mr. Vane also lies down to sleep in Adam's House of Dreams. Most of what he dreams is fairly self explanatory to most readers, although some may question lines such as:

> I was Adam, waiting for God to breath into my nostrils the breath of life. —I was not Adam, but a child in the bosom of a mother white with radiant whiteness. I was a youth on a white horse, leaping from cloud to cloud of a blue heaven....[35]

These are the kinds of thoughts wherewith we must tread lightly if we dare tread at all. MacDonald constantly, like all the mystics before him, asks himself the most primal question of life: What is real? And more deeply yet: What is reality? Whether we believe, like MacDonald and the majority of the mystics, that everything exists in the mind of God, or that everything is external to God's being, either way we face the same dilemma, the difficulty being that God still must sustain everything no matter where it lies in the region of existence(s). God is emanate to all things. He is the Absolute Reality that sustains the lesser created realities wherever their regions lie. Who is to say that all created beings exist in the same fashion or the same degree of realness? Or that everyone around us is just another human of the same sort as we ourselves? If God is the light in all things, then perhaps by design his light shines more brightly in some than in others. Possibly there are some vessels created for destruction as St. Paul suggests. But, are those vessels really of the same variety as ourselves? And if this be true in any measure at all, then might it not be said that God may manifest himself, or even our own selves, in not only different degrees and types, but in several at the same time? (keeping in mind that, as Einstein told us, time is an illusion of sorts). Can a person be more than one person at once? Can a person live in and out of timelines as more than one person, yet simultaneously in all of them? If God himself can be in all places and all things at once, why not his created beings if he so wills it?

Or is MacDonald simply suggesting that Mr. Vane is seeing the world in his dreams through the eyes of other beings, stepping into their skins so to speak? To many readers this may seem more sensible. However, we must remember that he often gave us characters that were more than one person. Perhaps the most memorable was the lead character in his fairytale, *The Wise Woman*, who appeared in many different forms within the story. "'But which is the real you?' asked Rosamond: 'This or that?'... 'Or a thousand others?', returned the wise woman." It's no good thinking that Mr. Vane was just dreaming so it wasn't *real* anyway. To George MacDonald there was no such thing as *just a dream*!

For those who appear to be at the deepest levels of mystical faith, the whole of creation seems for them to come down to only two beings really: themselves and what is commonly referred to as the "Holy Other", or the "Beloved" as Dante often called *It*. For mystics who constantly question what and who around them is real, it is the manifestation of the Beloved that keeps them from falling into total solipsism. The Holy Other may come in several forms throughout any given day, or every day. For Dante the Holy Other came in the form of a human woman named Beatrice. But the Beloved's presence may be felt in everything in some measure. MacDonald puts this beautifully in what may be his greatest fairytale for children, *The Golden Key*, when one of the story's main characters, a young girl named Tangle, descends what looks like an infinite stairway, which in turn leads into a cave deep within the Earth.

She saw no one in the cave. But the moment she stood upright she had a marvellous sense that she was in the secret of the earth and all its ways. Everything she had seen, or learned from books; all that her grandmother had said or sung to her; all the talk of the beasts, birds, and fishes; all that had happened to her on her journey with Mossy, and since then in the heart of the earth with the Old man and the Older man—all was plain: she understood it all, and saw that everything meant the same thing, though she could not have put it into words again.

The next moment she descried, in a corner of the cave, a little naked child, sitting on the moss. He was playing with balls of various colours and sizes, which he disposed in strange figures upon the floor beside him. And now Tangle felt that there was something in her knowledge which was not in her understanding. For she knew there must be an infinite meaning in the change and sequence and individual forms of the figures into which the child arranged the balls, as well as in the varied harmonies of their colours, but what it all meant she could not tell. ...Flashes of meaning would now pass from them to Tangle, and now again all would be not merely obscure, but utterly dark... an indescribable vague intelligence went on rousing itself in her mind. For seven years she had stood there watching the naked child with his coloured balls, and it seemed to her like seven hours, when all at once the shape the balls took, she knew not why, reminded her of the Valley of Shadows, and she spoke:—

"Where is the Old Man of the Fire?" she said.

"Here I am," answered the child, rising and leaving his balls on the moss.[36]

116

GEORGE MACDONALD

This budding consciousness of oneness between God and creation expressed in *The Golden Key*, and spattered throughout the latter portion of *Lilith*, as well as other of MacDonald's tales, may owe a great deal to the mystic, Julian of Norwhich. He sometimes quotes from her in a paraphrased way in *Lilith* or at least paraphrases some of her ideas. When Mr. Vane awakens for the final time in Adam's House of Death after many false awakenings, he asks Adam if he will have to die again? But Adam tells him that he has now died unto life and has "only to keep dead." This is a discussion on sin, Adam being unwavering in his manner of speech that Mr. Vane can keep from sinning, symbolized by his, "having to live", with all his, "blessed might", and yet Mr. Vane questions his own ability to stay strong in this. Eve tells him that all he needs is to have the will, and the strength will be with him, and that now it's all "...upwardness, and love and gladness." Then Mara adds, "What will be well, is even now well."[37] In the text of Julian's manuscript, *Showing of Love*, she had been distraught by the sinfulness present in creation and began to wonder why sin was ever allowed to come into the world. God answered her, "It behooved that there should be sin; but all shall be well, and all shall be well, and all manner of thing shall be well", and at this she began to see sin in a new light, as a beginning that had to be in order to bring about a greater end. And like Mr. Vane, this great Contemplative starts to see God in everything in some fashion or degree. Formerly, she, like so many of George MacDonald's main characters, had a hard time understanding how evil and beauty could exist in the same framework. In her case that framework was the whole of creation, whereas MacDonald quite often used beautiful, yet evil, women to show the same disparity.

Eventually Mr. Vane, Lona, and most of the children awaken and hear the crowing of the golden cock who for millions of years has "stood on the clock of the universe". It means the dawn of the new creation of which Revelation teaches. A short time later they leave the House of Dreams and begin their heavenward journey. On the way, they soon begin to realize that they have been changed, softened, marinated by restful sleep in Adam's house, and that because they've been changed, the world around them takes on a new meaning.

A wondrous change had passed upon the world—or was it not rather that a change more marvellous had taken place in us? Without light enough in the sky or the air to reveal anything, every heather-bush, every small shrub, every blade of grass was perfectly visible—either by light that went out from it, as fire from the bush Moses saw in the desert, or by light that went out of our eyes. Nothing cast a shadow; all things interchanged a little light. Every growing thing showed me, by its shape and colour, its indwelling idea—the informing thought, that is, which was its being, and sent it out. My bare feet seemed to love every plant they trod upon. The world and my being, its life and mine, were one. The microcosm and macrocosm were at length atoned, at length in harmony! I lived in everything; everything entered and lived in me. To be aware of a thing, was to know its life at once and mine, to know whence we came, and where we were at home—was to know that we are all what we are, because Another is what he is! Sense after sense, hitherto asleep, awoke in me—sense after sense indescribable ... When a little breeze brushing a bush of heather set its purple bells a ringing, I was myself in the joy of the bells, myself in the joy of the breeze to which responded their sweet tin-tinning,* myself in the joy of the sense, and of the soul that received all the joys together.[38]

118

GEORGE MACDONALD

The footnote in the passage indicated by the star after the phrase, "tin-tinning", gives us the Italian text of a quote from Dante's *Paradiso*:

> * Tin tin sonando con si dolce nota
> Che 'I ben disposto spirto d' amor turge. Del
> Paradiso, x. 142.

Rather than just translate the two lines MacDonald gives us, let's look at the entire stanza in this portion of *Paradiso*:

> Like a clock that calls us at the hour when the bride of God rises to sing matins to the Bridegroom that he may love her, when one part draws or drives another, sounding the chime with notes so sweet that the well-ordered spirit swells with love, so I saw the glorious wheel move and render voice to voice with harmony and sweetness that cannot be known but there where joy becomes eternal.[39]

A clock of the universe is instrumental in Dante's Divine Comedy, and MacDonald has been waving his arms and shouting, trying his best to point us to it throughout these last several passages.

When they come to the fearful hollow (Bad Burrow), they find now a much more peaceful lake and surrounding environment than ever they had encountered in their previous crossings. When we discussed Mr. Vane's first trip through the Bad Burrow much earlier in the book, it will be remembered that it was suggested how it seemed likely to symbolize the evil struggle going on in Lilith's mind. And later when Mr. Vane, Lona, Mara, and the children had left Mara's cottage and were crossing the Bad Burrow while headed for Adam's House of Dreams with Lilith in tow, they came to a lake in the burrow where Mr. Vane says to us:

Mara stepped into it; not a movement answered her tread or the feat of my horse. But the moment that the elephants carrying the princess touched it, the seemingly solid earth began to heave and boil, and the whole dread brood of the hellish nest was commoved. Monsters uprose on all sides, every neck at full length ... went out after Lilith.[40]

This time, however, while crossing the burrow and passing the lake, they find that the evil creatures are still in the lake but are lying motionless at its bottom.

I gazed into its pellucid depths. A whirl-pool had swept out the soil in which the abortions burrowed, and at the bottom lay visible the whole horrid brood ... they weltered in motionless heaps—shapes more fantastic in ghoulish, blasting dismay, than ever wine-sodden brain of exhausted poet fevered into misbeing. He who dived in the swirling Maelstrom[41] saw none to compare with them in horror ....

Not one of them moved as we passed. But they were not dead. So long as exist men and women of unwholesome mind, that lake will still be peopled with loathsomenesses.[42]

So now we know that the Bad Burrow and its lake full of terrible monsters, represents not only Lilith's mind/spirit, but the restless spirits of all mankind when they come into the world beyond the glass. But now that Lilith is dreaming and sleeping the good sleep, as had Mr. Vane, Lona, and the children, the Bad Burrow and lake representing their spirits is being calmed and set right, and this is the new heaven and the new earth. And needless to say, all the channels are now full of water since Lilith has let go of what was not hers to keep.

GEORGE MACDONALD

They walk through what used to be the desert region and find that it's now teaming with vegetation. Following on the banks of the river of life, they come to and pass through, a great forest only to find before their eyes that mountain we call Zion, with the New Jerusalem clinging to its surface. The river now looks so pristine that Mr. Vane comments that, only now has he seen "real water", and that every other water is only "like it". Everything during their journey has that same realness to it, so much so that the life they left behind seems only an imitation. C.S. Lewis seems to have borrowed this for his ending to the Narnia series, where the children who had died, followed Aslan through the real Narnia and saw that the old one they left behind was only a copy (a shadow). Those who have studied philosophy will recognize Plato's famous *Theory of Forms* in this train of thought.

To talk further of what the travelers saw and felt in that great city would be to no avail. MacDonald paints both an inner and outer picture of such rare beauty that tearing it into pieces for commentary would almost seem wicked. Onward we must go to the poignant conclusion of the tale.

After the women angels come to take the children away, (oddly Macdonald casts his angels here in both male and female form) Mr. Vane, with Lona by his side, passes through the city and begins the ascent to the throne of God. A throne, incidentally, that Mr. Vane can only see with inner vision, assumedly because God is something akin to a being of pure thought, and thus must be seen with the power of thought. During great flashes of light on the mountain, we get a glimpse into the creative mind of God in action, creating and sustaining all life from animals to angels and even Mr. Vane's mother. This would further add to our earlier conclusion that MacDonald believed everything existed within the mind of its Creator in some fashion that's impossible to comprehend. But, within heaven's shores, everything that is seen and touched and heard with the senses, is also felt with new senses indescribable in which one feels the very presence of God and knows His thoughts, sees through His eyes and heart what he has made, and feels the joy He feels in having made it. "I saw, not the intent alone, but the intender too; not the idea alone, but the imbodier present, the operant outsender...."[43]

But a strange thing happens when Mr. Vane reaches the top of the stairs.

> My heart beating with hope and desire, I held faster the hand of my Lona, and we began to climb; but soon we let each other go, to use hands as well as feet in the toilsome ascent of the huge stones. At length we drew near the cloud, which hung down the steps like the borders of a garment, passed through the fringe, and entered the deep folds. A hand, warm and strong, laid hold of mine, and drew me to a little door with a golden lock. The door opened; the hand let mine go, and pushed me gently through. I turned quickly, and saw the board of a large book in the act of closing behind me. I stood alone in my library.[44]

This ending of Mr. Vane's mystical journey may seem to some a disappointment, perhaps even cruel. MacDonald, however, used his stories as a platform to teach us his unique insights into spiritual matters. His son Ronald tells us that his father felt that, although denied a regular church pastorate, God had given him his writing skills to replace it with. He would not waste his gift simply to supply the reader with sentimentality. Instead he uses the finale to make two statements more. The first is a short discourse on the problems inherit within psychology. Freud and his contemporaries were already building a reputation at the turn of the 20th century that largely took advantage of the materialistic ideology that was by now in full steam. In another decade or so, G.K. Chesterton would be holding well publicized debates with H.G. Wells, Clarence

Darrow, and George Bernard Shaw on topics concerning religious belief. The psychological notion of mystical states of consciousness somehow magically being produced in our minds, *by our minds*, and without our knowledge of it, brought about dismay to the intellect of MacDonald. It brought scorn and laughter to the mind of Chesterton. But, much of the rest of the world seemed ready to accept such a proposal without question (and apparently without much thought). MacDonald addresses this topic while allowing Mr. Vane to have a conversation with his self. Or *was* it his self that he was conversing with?

In moments of doubt I cry,

"Could God Himself create such lovely things as I dreamed?"

"Whence then came thy dream?" answers Hope.

"Out of my dark self, into the light of my consciousness."

"But whence first into thy dark self?" rejoins Hope.

"My brain was its mother, and the fever in my blood its father."

"Say rather," suggests Hope, "thy brain was the violin whence it issued, and the fever in thy blood the bow that drew it forth.—But who made the violin? and who guided the bow across its strings? Say rather, again—who set the song birds each on its bough in the tree of life, and startled each in its order from its perch? Whence came the fantasia? and whence the life that danced thereto? Didst thou say, in the dark of thy own unconscious self, 'Let beauty be; let truth seem!' and straightway beauty was, and truth but seemed?"

Man dreams and desires; God broods and wills and quickens.

C.S. LEWIS CALLED HIM MASTER

When a man dreams his own dream, he is the sport of his dream; when Another gives it him, that Other is able to fulfill it.[45]

Let us remember that MacDonald wrote this great work at the turn of that century where Spiritualism, along with its comrades, occultism and magic, were being practiced at an all-time high throughout both America and Great Britain. It held a particular attraction for writers of the day; from Tennyson to Sir Arthur Conan Doyle, but also for society at large; from American First Lady, Mary Lincoln, to British Prime Minister, William Gladstone. It was also being examined by some of MacDonald's closest friends (much to his chagrin), such as Lady Cowper-Temple and John Ruskin. On *Lilith's* final pages, MacDonald preaches his staunchest warning yet to occultists who would like to knock down the doors that bar us from forbidden worlds rather than wait to be drawn in by the power of God.

I have never again sought the mirror. The hand sent me back: I will not go out again by that door! "All the days of my appointed time will I wait till my change come." [Quoting Job 14:14]

Now and then, when I look round on my books, they seem to waver as if a wind rippled their solid mass, and another world were about to break through. Sometimes when I am abroad, a like thing takes place; the heavens and the earth, the trees and the grass appear for a moment to shake as if about to pass away; then, lo, they have settled again into the old familiar face! At times I seem to hear whisperings around me, as if some that loved me were talking of me; but when I would distinguish the words, they cease, and all is very still. I know not whether these things rise in my brain, or enter it from without. I do not seek them; they come, and I let them go.[46]

The mysticism of Mr. Vane, and the only mysticism George MacDonald will allow for in the life of a Christian, is one that comes with a large dose of self restraint. "I wait; asleep or awake, I wait", he says. The kind of spiritual adventure that occurred in the life of Mr. Vane should not be expected by all Christians. Nor should those who undergo such an experience be thought of as more blessed than others. MacDonald might also have added the refrain, "Blessed are those who have not seen and yet believed". Among the central attainments that Mr. Vane took from his explorations were patience, self restraint, and forbearance—the very things he least expected to come away with when he started his journey. If hell is getting what you want until you're sick of it, as C.S. Lewis once suggested, perhaps heaven, at least in some measure, is getting what you least expect.

Lilith is a marvel of English literature. There's never been anything like it in the least except for MacDonald's own *Phantastes* completed some forty years earlier. And while neither book has ever had the wide following most of the author's fans would have hoped for, it could well be that these books were only meant to be read and comprehended by a select few. MacDonald probably wouldn't have had it any other way.

Chapter 6
The Devil Has His Day

George MacDonald might have done a good many other things with his life had there been more time to do them. He was a pretty fair carpenter and a fine leather worker. One of his hobbies was making new bindings for old books. In his younger years, despite his damaged lungs, he was said to have been quite an athlete—a swift and cunning boxer. Starting in the mid 1870's, he was able to live in Italy during the winter months. This did wonders for his lungs and brought new vigor to him. Michael Phillips has included in his reprint of Ronald MacDonald's essay on his father, a photograph taken on or slightly before 1879 (Maurice is in the picture and he died that year) of George MacDonald with several of his sons standing against a rocky hillside, and although in his late forties, Macdonald still looks like the best athlete in the bunch, with an obvious boxer's build about him. (Incidentally, Wilfred Dodgson, the brother of Lewis Carroll, taught MacDonald's daughter, Mary, to box). He could read German, French, Italian, Dutch, Greek, Latin, and Spanish and could have easily spent his days immersed in translator's work. His first published literary effort was a translation of the

GEORGE MACDONALD

German poems of Novalis which MacDonald published himself in a small run for friends and family in 1851. In 1876 Strahan published his translations again of Novalis along with songs and poems by Luther, Heine, Goethe, and others from both German and Italian. MacDonald had two thorns in his side: bad lungs due to constant bouts with bronchitis and asthma which made physical labor difficult, and the complete lack of common sense among those who sat in positions of authority at the church he was pastor of for such a short time, and it was because of these adversities that he became a writer. Sometimes a thorn is nothing more than a much needed push from the Father.

But, despite his success as a writer, MacDonald would struggle financially most of his life. There was a split in the ownership of one of his publishers, after which, despite selling more of them now, he found that he could not get nearly as much for his books as he had years earlier. He would outlive his wife, four of his eleven children, even some of his grandchildren. The deaths of his wife, and his daughter, Lily, particularly traumatized him. Yet he would always talk of how very little adversity he had faced in his life, as though he were specially blessed among men. His final years would have a bleakness in them however. His mind became increasingly foggy, and he stopped writing altogether in 1897. About this same time, he came down with a severe skin disease that was so painful he could barely sleep for at least two full years. It's not known exactly what occurred, some think it was a stroke, but around 1900 he lost his ability to talk and never regained it. The only blessing it seemed was that, with the loss of his voice, his skin conditioned cleared up, he was able to sleep again, and his mind became brighter. Still, he quietly awaited his death, seldom leaving the house for the last seven years of his natural life. But, though full of sadness, he never lost his faith that there was a greater good coming to him—something too good for him to know. Greville tells us that he appeared to be waiting for his wife to come through the door one final time to take him to his true home, and that whenever anyone came to the house, he would look up with anxious eyes to see who it was, and once having seen that it was not his beloved Louisa, would let out a sigh and go back to his vigil. One cannot help but be reminded of the closing words of *Lilith* through the voice of Mr. Vane as he looks forward to his time of departure when he will see his Lona once again. "I wait; asleep or awake, I wait... Novalis says, 'Our life is no dream, but it should and will perhaps become one.'"[1]

George MacDonald went to his rest at nearly eighty one years of age, September 18, 1905, and while much of his contemporary Scotland doted on his novels during his lifetime, many years later through influential authors like G.K. Chesterton and C.S. Lewis, it was his fantasy stories—his fairytales for children and adults alike—that would finally take the forefront in the public's admiration just as he believed they eventually would. A centenary celebration was held in 1924 in honor of what would have been George MacDonald's one hundredth birthday. G.K. Chesterton was chairman of the event. While a program survives showing the featured speakers and singers, some of them MacDonald's own sons and daughters, we have no transcription of all the wonderful speeches and anecdotes that must have been presented that day. We can imagine though that Chesterton's wit would have been at full throttle, and he might well have at some point given a humorous talk on the importance of fairy stories such as this from his essay, *The Dragon's Grandmother*.

> I listened to what he said about the society politely enough, I hope; but when he incidentally mentioned that he did not believe in fairy tales, I broke out beyond control. "Man," I said, "who are you that you should not believe in fairy tales? It is much easier to believe in Blue Beard than to believe in you. A blue beard is a

misfortune; but there are green ties which are sins. It is far easier to believe in a million fairy tales than to believe in one man who does not like fairy tales. I would rather kiss Grimm instead of a Bible and swear to all his stories as if they were thirty-nine articles than say seriously and out of my heart that there can be such a man as you; that you are not some temptation of the devil or some delusion from the void. Look at these plain, homely, practical words. 'The Dragon's Grandmother,' that is all right; that is rational almost to the verge of rationalism. If there was a dragon, he had a grandmother. But you— you had no grandmother! If you had known one, she would have taught you to love fairy tales. You had no father, you had no mother; no natural causes can explain you. You cannot be. I believe many things which I have not seen; but of such things as you it may be said, 'Blessed is he that has seen and yet has disbelieved.'"[2]

Endnotes

Chapter 1

1. From William Shakespeare's play, *The Tempest*, Act IV, scene 1.
2. E.T.A. Hoffman's novel, *The Devil's Elixirs*, originally published by Blackwood & Cadell, 1824. The edition used for this book is Trans.: Ronald Taylor, J. Calder, London, 1963, (from the "Introduction").
3. GMD's essay, "The Fantastic Imagination", originally published in: *Dish of Orts*, 1893. The edition used for this book is: Sampson Low Marston & Co, London, Great Britain, 1895.
4. Ibid.
5. From Friedrich Hollander's cabaret, *Munchhausen*.
6. G.K. Chesterton, *Orthodoxy*, Dodd, Mead & Company, New York, NY, 1908, pp. 46-47.
7. Greville MacDonald, *George MacDonald and his Wife*, George Allen & Company, London, Great Britain, 1924, p. 9. (from the "Introduction", written by G.K. Chesterton).
8. Ibid., p. 13.

GEORGE MACDONALD
Chapter 2

1. C.S. Lewis, *George MacDonald: An Anthology*, Macmillan Publishing Company, New York, NY, 1947, p. xxxii-iii. (from the "Preface").
2. GMD, *Phantastes*, Smith, Elder & Company, London, Great Britain, 1858, p. 3.
3. Ibid., p. 69.
4. Greville MacDonald, *George MacDonald and his Wife*, p. 109.
5. Ibid., p. 124.
6. GMD, *Unspoken Sermons*, Volume 3—"Life".
7. GMD, *Phantastes*, p. 76.
8. Ibid., p. 77.
9. Ibid., p. 85.
10. Ibid., p. 88.
11. Ibid., p. 89.
12. Ibid., pp. 84-85.
13. Ibid., p. 95.
14. Ibid., pp. 91-92.
15. GMD, *The Portent* (A Story Of The Inner Vision Of The Highlanders Commonly Called The Second Sight), Harper & Row Publishers Inc., New York, NY, 1979, p. 45. *The Portent* was originally published as a 3-part story in Cornhill Magazine, 1860, May—*Its Legend*, June—*The Omen Coming On*, July—*The Omen Fulfilled*.
16. From Novalis's Poem Collection, *Hymn's to the Night*, selection number 4, translated by GMD.
17. GMD, *Phantastes*, p. 117.
18. Ibid., p. 125.
19. Ibid., p. 184.
20. GMD's essay, *The Fantastic Imagination*.
21. Ibid.

C.S. LEWIS CALLED HIM MASTER

Chapter 3

1. Greville MacDonald, *George MacDonald and his Wife*, p. 116.

2. GMD, *Alec Forbes of Howglen*, Hurst & Blackett Publishers, London, Great Britain, 1865, p. 157.

3. C.S. Lewis gives a wonderful apologetic in Chapter 16 of his book, *Miracles*, concerning why he thought the world began to change at the resurrection of Jesus, and how those who are followers of his should also begin to change, and, not only become morally superior to what they were before, but also that they should, like all of nature, gradually become a new kind of being with attributes that could, and should, seem miraculous to the old kind of being. That Christ was not a one of a kind hominid, but rather, the prototype hominid, whose seemingly miraculous acts that often took place somehow beyond nature itself, would serve as an example of what is only the beginning of a great change in many people to come.

4. Greville MacDonald, *George MacDonald and his Wife*, p. 298.

5. From a fragment of Novalis's essay — *Of the Secret World*.

6. G.K. Chesterton, *Autobiography*, Hutchinson, London, Great Britain, 1936, pp. 49-50.

7. Greville MacDonald, *George MacDonald and his Wife*, p. 78.

8. Ibid., p. 80.

9. Ibid., p. 84.

10. Interestingly, author, Charles Walter Stansby Williams, (possibly influenced by GMD's — *Lilith*) never referred to any of his characters using *their* imagination. They would simply talk of using — imagination — as though it were a vast well that everyone had access to, rather than each individual having their own. That may sound Jungian on a surface level, but I seriously doubt that Jung had the vaguest notion of what this other world where imagination lay was truly about or what it meant to a mystic. Williams obviously did.

11. GMD's essay, *The Fantastic Imagination*.

12. From Ronald MacDonald's essay, "George MacDonald: A Personal Note". This article first appeared in 1911 within the pages of a book consisting of nine essays from various authors on Scottish topics. The book was entitled, *From a Northern Window: Papers, Critical, Historical and Imaginative,* James Nesbet & Company, London, Great Britain, 1911. Ronald's wonderful, but short, essay (only 58-pages) appeared as the third chapter. The book is long out of print; however, Michael Phillips repackaged the essay as a solo book in 1989 under the title: *From a Northern Window: A Personal Reminiscence of George MacDonald by his Son.* It was published by Sunrise Books, Eureka, CA, 1989. As of this writing the book is listed as out of print, but a used copy may be easily found.

13. GMD, *The Poetical Works of George MacDonald,* Volume 1—Violin Songs, "Faith".

14. Greville MacDonald, *George MacDonald and his Wife,* pp. 457-58.

15. Ibid., p. 424.

16. Ronald MacDonald's essay, *George MacDonald: A Personal Note.*

17. GMD, *Unspoken Sermons,* Volume 3—"The Creation in Christ".

18. Greville MacDonald, *George MacDonald and his Wife,* p. 174.

Chapter 4

1. GMD's article, "Browning's Christmas Eve", published in the *Christian Spectator,* May, 1853.

2. I don't know what GMD actually thought of the virgin birth and only mention it as a demonstrative event, the likes of which, would parallel his thinking on similar biblical issues.

3. GMD, *Unspoken Sermons,* Volume 3—"Justice".

4. Greville MacDonald, *George MacDonald and his Wife,* p. 118.

5. John Calvin, *Institutes,* 3. 21. 5.

6. GMD, *Weighed and Wanting*, Samson & Low, London, Great Britain, 1882, Page 47.

7. GMD, *Alec Forbes of Howglen*, P. 85.

8. Greville MacDonald, *George MacDonald and his Wife*, p. 132.

9. Ibid., pp. 373-74.

10. Ronald MacDonald's essay, *George MacDonald: A Personal Note*.

Chapter 5

1. On a very selfish side note let me say that, many years before I ever read anything by MacDonald, I had a vivid dream where I met God, and in this dream I was in a room that seemed to be without end, and which was filled with beds, and men to sleep on them. It was not part of this life or physical world but apparently a spirit world, perhaps after death. God then took me back in time to a different Earth. It is truly amazing how many people I've come across who seem to have had a similar dream or vision of being in an endless room filled with people in a spirit world. Reading *Lilith* for the first time left me breathless.

2. GMD, *Lilith*, Chatto & Windus, London, United Kingdom, 1895, pp. 39-40.

3. In 1927 John Dunne set out to prove what many people had proposed for thousands of years—that dreams often show us the future. He tested many, many students at Oxford University by having them write down their dreams and look to see if any part of them would come true during the coming days. His evidence that some (not all) people do indeed dream about future events on a semi-regular basis was very convincing. He wrote the now classic book, *An Experiment With Time*, in 1927 which chronicled his work. Both C.S. Lewis and J.R.R. Tolkien thought he had offered "proof" of his argument. Lewis referred to Dunne in at least five of his books. Whether MacDonald has

his Mr. Vane dreaming of seeing Lilith in the future is quite possible, but only conjecture.

4. GMD, *Lilith*, pp. 52-53.

5. Ibid., pp. 53-54.

6. Ibid., p. 92.

7. Ibid., p. 93.

8. Ibid., p. 93-94.

9. Ibid., p. 86.

10. Ibid., p. 64-65.

11. Ibid., p. 71.

12. Ibid., p. 141-42.

13. Ibid., p. 146.

14. From Samuel Taylor Coleridge's poem, *Kubla Khan*.

15. GMD, *Lilith*, p. 116.

16. The name is a bit of a misnomer as the gardens didn't really hang from anything in ancient Babylon. Rather, they were displayed on rooftops and atop of walls.

17. GMD, *Lilith*, p. 243.

18. Ibid., p. 21.

19. Ibid., p. 16.

20. Ibid., p. 15.

21. Ibid., p. 231.

22. Greville MacDonald, *George MacDonald and his Wife*, p. 554.

23. GMD, *Lilith*, pp. 147-48.

24. G.K. Chesterton, *The Ball and the Cross*, Wells Gardner, Danton & Company, Ltd., London, 1910 p. 178.

25. Greville mentions in his biography of his father that, George MacDonald wrote a letter in 1875, apparently from Mr. and Mrs. Cowper Temple's home at Broadlands where he sometimes spent the night, telling of how there was a woman there, a medium, (unidentified except as Mrs. A.), who described a scene where Rose La Touche was whispering something to Ruskin. She described Rose apparently very well without ever having seen her, to the point of convincing Ruskin that her clairvoyant abilities were real enough. Rose La Touche,

Ruskin's greatest love interest, had just died that year. Both La Touche and Ruskin suffered from bouts of mental illness. Ruskin had what was likely his worst breakdown later during this year. He also tried desperately to finish his autobiography during this time, and in it he described the meeting with the clairvoyant as a "séance". MacDonald mentions nothing of a séance in the portion of the letter Greville printed and it would be arrogant on our part to assume George MacDonald was even present during the séance, let alone took part in it. This is especially true in light of the fact that he said of Mrs. A., "I don't take to her much", in the letter. It is a curious question however.

26. GMD, *Lilith*, p. 23.

27. Ibid., pp. 203-04.

28. Ibid., pp. 205-06.

29. Charles Williams, *Descent Into Hell*, Eerdmans, Grand Rapids, Michigan, 2001, pp. 221-22.

30. GMD, *Lilith*, pp. 207-08.

31. Ibid., p. 218.

32. Ibid., p. 219.

33. Ibid., p. 219.

34. Ibid., p. 218.

35. Ibid., pp. 230-31.

36. GMD, "The Golden Key", a short story/fairytale. This was first published in his collection of five fairy stories in the single volume—*Dealings With the Fairies*, Strahan, London, Great Britain, 1867. It can now be found in an assortment of other books containing MacDonald's children's stories. The one I used, and of which is still available as of this writing is, *The Gifts of the Christ Child & Other Stories and Fairy Tales*, Wm. B. Eerdmans Publishing Company, Grand Rapids, Michigan, 1973.

37. GMD, *Lilith*, p. 239.

38. Ibid., p. 243.

39. Dante, *Paradiso*, vv. 139-48.

40. GMD, *Lilith*, p. 211.

41. This is probably a reference to Edgar Allan Poe's 1841 short story, *A Descent Into the Maelstrom*, where an old sailor tells the story of how he and his brother aboard their ship were once sucked down into a whirlpool. The man had jumped off the ship thinking it might be better for him than being attached to it as it sunk, but before he does, he takes a good look at all the things he sees swirling in this great vortex which had been present in the sea for apparently many years and was legendary among sailors.
42. GMD, *Lilith*, p. 244.
43. Ibid., p. 250.
44. Ibid., p. 250.
45. Ibid., p. 251.
46. Ibid., pp. 251-52.

Chapter 6

1. GMD, *Lilith*, p. 252.
2. G.K. Chesterton, *Tremendous Trifles*, Dodd, Mead and Company, New York, New York, 1915, Chapter 16—"The Dragon's Grandmother".

George MacDonald: A Bibliography

The following is from Ronald MacDonald's essay/book, From a Northern Window:

"In a literary life of some forty-two years George MacDonald Produced some fifty-two volumes, of which twenty-five may be classed as novels, three as prose fantasies, eight as tales and allegories for children, five as sermons, three as literary and miscellaneous critical essays, and three as collections of short stories; and five volumes of verse, the greater part of which, with many poems gathered from the pages of the prose works, arranged in two volumes and finally revised by his own hand, was reissued in 1893."

A few of the following are collections in which some of the same works appear more than once.

GEORGE MACDONALD

1855, *Within and Without, a Poem*, Longmans, Brown, Green.

1857, *Poems*, Longmans, Brown, Green.

1858, *Phantastes* (A Faerie Romance for Men and Women), Smith, Elder.

1863, *David Elginbrod*, Hurst & Blackett.

1864, *Adela Cathcart*, Hurst & Blackett.

1864, *The Portent* (A Story Of The Inner Vision Of The Highlanders Commonly Called The Second Sight), Smith Elder

1865, *Alec Forbes of Howglen*, Hurst & Blackett.

1867, *Annals of a Quiet Neighbourhood*, Hurst & Blackett.

1867, *Dealings with the Fairies*, Strahan.

1867, *The Disciple and other Poems*, Strahan.

1867, *Unspoken Sermons, 1st Series*, Strahan.

1885, *Unspoken Sermons, 2nd Series*, Longmans, Green.

1889, *Unspoken Sermons, 3rd Series*, Longmans, Green.

1888, *Guild Court*, Hurst & Blackett.

1868, *Robert Falconer*, Hurst & Blackett.

C.S. LEWIS CALLED HIM MASTER

1868, *The Seaboard Parish*, Tinsley Bros.

1870, *The Miracles of our Lord*, Strahan.

1871, *At the Back of the North Wind*, Strahan.

1871, *Ranald Bannerman's Boyhood*, Strahan.

1871, *Works of Fancy and Imagination*, (chiefly reprints in several volumes), Chatto & Windus.

1872, *The Princess and the Goblin*, Strahan.

1872, *The Vicar's Daughter*, Tinsley Bros.

1872, *Wilfrid Cumbermede*, Hurst & Blackett.

1873, *Gutta Percha Willie* (The Working Genius), Henry S. King.

1874, *England's Antiphon*, Macmillan.

1875, *Malcolm*, Henry S. King.

1875, *The Wise Woman* (A Parable), Strahan.

1876, *Thomas Wingfold, Curate*, Hurst & Blackett.

1876, *St. George and St. Michael*, Henry S. King.

1876, *Exotics: A Translation (in verse) of the Spiritual Songs of Novalis, the Hymn Book of Luther and other Poems from the German and Italian*, Strahan.

1877, *The Marquis of Lossie*, Hurst & Blackett.

GEORGE MACDONALD

1879, *Sir Gibbie*, Hurst & Blackett.

1879, *Paul Faber, Surgeon*, Hurst & Blackett.

1880, *A Book of Strife, in the form of the Diary of an Old Soul*, Printed privately.

1881, *Mary Marston*, Sampson Low.

1882, *Castle Warlock, A Homely Romance*, Sampson Low.

1882, *Weighed and Wanting*, Sampson Low.

1882, *The Gifts of the Christ Child, and other Tales*, Sampson Low.

1882, *Orts*, Sampson Low.

1893, *A Dish of Orts* (an enlarged edition of Orts), Sampson Low.

1883, *Donal Grant*, Kegan Paul.

1883, *A Threefold Cord* (Poems by Three Friends), edited by George MacDonald, Printed privately.

1883, *The Princess and Curdie*, Chatto & Windus.

1885, *The Tragedie of Hamlet* (with a study of the text of the Folio of 1623), Longmans, Green.

1886, *What's Mine's Mine*, Kegan Paul.

1887, *Home Again*, a Tale, Kegan Paul.

1888, *The Elect Lady*, Kegan Paul.

C.S. LEWIS CALLED HIM MASTER

1886, *Cross Purposes, and The Shadows: Two Fairy Stories*, (reprinted from *Dealings with the Fairies*), Blackie & Sons.

1890, *A Rough Shaking, a Tale*, Blackie & Sons.

1891, *There and Back*, Kegan Paul.

1891, *The Flight of the Shadow*, Kegan Paul.

1891, *A Cabinet of Gems* (Cut and polished by Sir Philip Sidney, now for their more radiance presented without their setting by George MacDonald), Elliot Stock.

1892, *The Hope of the Gospel*, Ward, Lock, Bowden.

1893, *Heather and Snow*, Chatto & Windus.

1895, *Lilith*, a Romance, Chatto & Windus.

1897, *Rampolli: Growths from a Long-planted Root, being translations chiefly from the German, along with A Year's Diary of an Old Soul* (Poems), Longmans, Green.

1897, *Salted with Fire*, a Tale, Hurst & Blackett.

1893, *Poetical Works of George MacDonald*, (Mostly reprints but MacDonald modified many of the poems) Chatto & Windus.